WHY DID

JESUS

HAVE TO DIE?

It's not what you think!

CHRIS CONRAD

Scriptures taken from the Holy Bible, New International Version®, NIV®. Copyright © 1973, 1978, 1984, 2011 by Biblica, Inc.™ Used by permission of Zondervan. All rights reserved worldwide. www.zondervan.com The "NIV" and "New International Version" are trademarks registered in the United States Patent and Trademark Office by Biblica, Inc.™ All rights reserved.

ISBN: 978-1-4834-0938-2 (sc)
ISBN: 978-1-4834-0940-5 (hc)
ISBN: 978-1-4834-0939-9 (e)

Library of Congress Control Number: 2014904433

Because of the dynamic nature of the Internet, any web addresses or links contained in this book may have changed since publication and may no longer be valid. The views expressed in this work are solely those of the author and do not necessarily reflect the views of the publisher, and the publisher hereby disclaims any responsibility for them.

Any people depicted in stock imagery provided by Thinkstock are models, and such images are being used for illustrative purposes only. Certain stock imagery © Thinkstock.

Lulu Publishing Services rev. date: 04/27/2016

I am the way, the truth, and the life; no man cometh
unto the Father but by Me. (John 14:6, KJV)

I and the Father are one. (John 10:30, NIV)

Anyone who has seen Me, has seen the Father. (John 14:9, NIV)

I say not unto you that I will pray the Father for you. No,
the Father Himself loves you. (John 16:26–27, NIV)

And this is eternal life, that they may know You, the only true
God, and Jesus Christ whom You have sent. (John 17:3, NIV)

For I did not come to judge the world but to
save the world. (John 12:47, RSV)

Do not think that I shall accuse you to the Father; there is one who
accuses you—Moses, in whom you trust. (John 5:45, NKJV)

I am not ashamed of the gospel. For in it the righteousness
of God is revealed. (Rom. 1:16–17, RSV)

I no longer call you servants, because a servant
does not know his master's business. Instead, I
have called you friends. (John 15:15, NIV)

The Lord hardened Pharaoh's heart. (Exod. 20:10, NIV)
Pharaoh hardened his heart. (Exod. 8:32, KJV)

So Saul took his own sword and fell on it. (1 Sam. 31:4, NIV)
So the Lord put him to death [Saul]. (1 Chron. 10:14, KJV)

For God so loved the world that He gave His only
begotten Son, that whoever believes in Him should not
perish but have everlasting life. (John 3:16, KJV)

How can I give you up …? How can I hand
you over, Israel? (Hosea 11:8, NIV)

"Who of us can dwell with the consuming fire? Who of
us can dwell with everlasting burning?" Those who walk
righteously and speak what is right. (Isa. 33:14–15, NIV)

Contents

Preface ix

Part 1: Chronology

Chapter 1: Why are things this way? 1
Chapter 2: The Devil's Accusations 7
Chapter 3: How Can You Trust a God as Described? 19
Chapter 4: Great Controversy Perspective 21
Chapter 5: The Answer Gets Blurred 23
Chapter 6: God Hints at the Plan of Salvation—the Gospel 27
Chapter 7: Cain to the Flood 32
Chapter 8: The Flood—What Happens If You Fear God? 35
Chapter 9: The Covenants 37
Chapter 10: Abraham's Life and Called a Friend 40
Chapter 11: Abraham to the Exodus 45
Chapter 12: The Ten Commandments 49
Chapter 13: The Ten Commandments Accomplish 52
Chapter 14: The Ten Commandments—Misnomer 54
Chapter 15: God Added Rules 56
Chapter 16: Lessons of Trust 59
Chapter 17: Moses 62
Chapter 18: Joshua 64
Chapter 19: Judges 66
Chapter 20: A Kingdom Divided 68
Chapter 21: The Kingdom Splits 70
Chapter 22: Success? 73
Chapter 23: Going Home 76
Chapter 24: Intertestament Period 80
Chapter 25: The First-Century Jews 84
Chapter 26: Jesus Answers Questions 87
Chapter 27: The Author Comes to Explain 89

Chapter 28: Arbitrary, Exacting, Unforgiving, and Severe 95
Chapter 29: Did Jesus Explain the Sinner's Death? 108
Chapter 30: Two More Demonstrations.................................124

Part 2: Train Wrecks

Chapter 31: Three Train Wrecks....................................133
Chapter 32: Satan's Train Wreck....................................137
Chapter 33: The Traditional Train Wreck............................140

Part 3: Clarification

Chapter 34: Alternative Endings....................................149
Chapter 35: Healing..152
Chapter 36: Faith 154
Chapter 37: Aids to Faith 158
Chapter 38: God's Use of Law 165
Chapter 39: Emergency Measures 171
Chapter 40: Is It Legal?...177
Chapter 41: Know 180
Chapter 42: A New Perspective on Romans 183
Chapter 43: Fiery Furnace 193
Chapter 44: Rest...199
Chapter 45: Conclusion 201

Part 4: Definitions

Chapter 46: The Gospel...207
Chapter 47: Sin 209
Chapter 48: Wrath and Paraditimy (To Deliver) 212
Chapter 49: Words from Jesus 218

Works Cited..**221**
Suggested Reading and Sources 227
About the Author...229

Preface

After writing a book for church leaders, I was asked to write another that discussed the same general topics for people who were not as familiar with all of the Bible stories, people who loved God and wanted a clear explanation of why it is that we are righteous by faith. I hope that once you have finished reading this book, you can agree that trust is all God has ever asked of His family and understand why this is true.

For the purpose of this book, you can assume all the Bible quotations are from the 1984 edition of the New International Version, unless shown otherwise, and all **bold** and *italic* print is my added emphasis, designed to draw your attention to certain words or phrases of the quoted author. Also, the terms Great Controversy Model, Demonstration Model, Natural Consequences, and Trust Healing Models—or any combination of these—should be considered synonymous, with only slight differences in emphasis.

I'd like to say thanks to Randy, Scott, Steve, Ahmed, and Marvin, friends who have encouraged me in this effort. I also want to acknowledge the impact of Pine Knolls, Graham Maxwell, and those we have learned from in the past.

Part 1

Chronology

CHAPTER 1

Why are things this way?

I n your mind's eye, look outside your door and peer into the ghettos and dark alleys of this world. In your heart, you know this is not what God had in mind for our planet. Sure, there is good out there, but there is bad too. There is beauty in bright smiles and romantic sunsets, blue oceans and painted deserts, quasars and star-studded skies, but there is ugliness in disease, decay, and death. And there is pain, a lot of pain. Why are things this way? Why do lions and tigers eat Bambi and Thumper? Why are the good often bad and the bad sometimes good? Why does the song say, "Only the good die young"? And why did someone as loving as Jesus have to die?

Many people have offered answers to that question. Some explanations revolve around some type of ransom being paid to the devil; others say that Jesus paid a debt to His Father, to the angels, or to sin itself. Are these the only options? Has the question been adequately addressed? Why is it that no earthly court would ever allow some saintly fellow to take the punishment for a criminal, yet many religions think it is okay for God to do so? Could punishing Gandhi ever atone for Hitler's crimes? Could Mother Teresa's virtue ever negate the lack thereof in Stalin, Pol Pot, Nero, Hirohito, or Osama bin Laden?

Surely it is arrogant to suggest that humanity has exhausted all the possibilities or that we could actually comprehend it all. So with that, I would like to throw one more possibility into the theological hat for consideration: the Great Controversy-Demonstration Model. Several people have incorporated great controversy concepts into their theology, but none have risen to the heights of Dr. Graham Maxwell, Ph.D University of Chicago. Many of the ideas presented here were first learned from this great man.

This book is divided into four sections. The first is historic, tracing the biblical story to the cross. The second is allegorical, using train-wreck metaphors to compare theologies. The third section looks at issues one by one, and section four defines terms.

Ephesus

To begin, let's go on a quick journey to Ephesus, the ancient metropolis located just off the Aegean Sea in modern-day Turkey. The year is AD 90, fifty-seven years after the crucifixion of Jesus and only twenty years after the Roman general Titus Augustus and his lieutenant, Tiberius Alexander, besieged Jerusalem. Their men set the city on fire, torched the temple, and melted the golden vessels into the tiny cracks of the marble floor, all out of hatred. In total, they slaughtered over a million Jewish men, women, and children.

Emperor Domitian reigns over the Roman Empire, and Ephesus is second only to Rome in power and is the seat of government in Asia Minor. It is home to almost five hundred thousand Romans, Greeks, Jews, and a dwindling number of Christians. The temple of Artemis (Diana) is there, and the city will soon have the world's largest outdoor theater, seating close to twenty-four thousand spectators. There are marble bathhouses, concrete aqueducts, and monstrous granite buildings everywhere. The city emulates Rome.

Though the city is ramping up its commerce and culture, the Christian church is diving, losing members and influence. Its once-courageous leaders are getting old, and those who knew the apostles are dying off. Corrupt leaders are circulating deceptive letters, splintering the church. And because of the recent beatings, members are leaving in droves.

That is what Ephesus was like when Tychicus found out. Dust and gravel fly from under his sandals as he bolts out the door. Racing down cobblestone streets, he weaves his way to the city square and, like a chameleon, blends into the crowd. He visits street venders and open markets. In whispers, he tells them, "Tomorrow noon, there's a meeting at my house." The word spreads throughout the city.

They walk the narrow, cobbled streets leading to Tychicus's house, remembering the beating they got for going to the last meeting. And though it has been awhile, remembering Paul's decapitation and Peter's upside-down crucifixion still stands their hair on end. And John, the last living disciple, is about to die on the barren rock of an island called Patmos. Rumor has it he was boiled in oil before being sent to prison. One thought is on their minds: *What has happened to the promise?*

Stuffed like a turkey into the single-roomed stucco, all sixty or so wait with bated breath. A distinguished muscular man and his younger brother begin to roll out a twenty-foot-long leather scroll, and the older of the two men starts to read:

The revelation of Jesus Christ, which God gave him to show his servants what must soon take place. He made it known by sending his angel to his servant John, who testifies to everything he saw—that is, the word of God and the testimony of Jesus Christ. Blessed is the one who reads the words of this prophecy, and blessed are those who hear it and take to heart what is written in it, because the time is near.

John, to the seven churches in the province of Asia:

Grace and peace to you from him who is, and who was, and who is to come, and from the seven spirits before his throne, and from Jesus Christ, who is the faithful witness, the firstborn from the dead, and the ruler of the kings of the earth. To him who loves us and has freed us from our sins by his blood, and has made us to be a kingdom and priests to serve his God and Father—to him be glory and power for ever and ever! Amen. Look, he is coming with the clouds, and every eye will see him, even those who pierced him; and all the peoples of the earth will mourn because of him. So shall it be! Amen. "I am the Alpha and the Omega," says the Lord God, "who is, and who was, and who is to come, the Almighty."

No paragraphs, verses, punctuation, or even spaces separate the Greek words they read from right to left. The men take turns reading, switching places every five minutes or so. They read about churches, candlesticks, beasts, trumpets, scorpions, grasshoppers, what appears to be a flying carpet or scroll, and a monstrous red dragon.

Then another sign appeared in heaven: an enormous red dragon with seven heads and ten horns and seven crowns on its heads. Its tail swept a third of the stars out of the sky and flung them to the earth. The dragon stood in front of the woman who was about to give birth, so that it might devour her child the moment he was born. She gave birth to a son, a male child, who "will rule all the nations with an iron scepter." And her child was snatched up to God and to his throne. The woman fled into the wilderness to a place prepared for her by God, where she might be taken care of for 1,260 days.

Then war broke out in heaven. Michael and his angels fought against the dragon, and the dragon and his angels fought back. But he was not strong enough, and they lost their place in heaven. The great dragon was hurled down—that ancient serpent called the devil, or Satan, who leads the whole world astray. He was hurled to the earth, and his angels with him. (Rev. 12:3–9)

It takes about an hour to read the letter, but they don't quit until they have finished the last line: "He who testifies to these things says, 'Yes, I am coming soon.' Amen. Come, Lord Jesus. The grace of the Lord Jesus be with God's people. Amen" (Rev. 22:20–21).

The crowd disperses as quickly as it came, with everyone taking different routes home. With skin tingling they discuss what they just heard.

"Is that what you expected?"

"No way. I've never heard anything like that! And I'd like to hear it again. But it is clear that Jesus really would like to come back but can't. There must be some gigantic issues we don't know about. It sounds to me like millions of lives are at stake. And it is complicated."

"That letter is exactly what I needed to hear. I can see history and prophesy falling into place. Now I know what Paul was saying in his letters. Now I feel like I can go on. I know someday He'll come back."

And they did go on. The Christian church has endured for over two thousand years and has thrived, converting billions of people to the faith. And that Revelation message, though it was written to the seven churches of Asia Minor, is exactly what we need to hear today so we can go on, because we are still waiting and wondering too.

Why hasn't Jesus come back like He promised? Why is our world in such a mess? The Bible says it has to do with a war, and we are all in it.

CHAPTER 2

The Devil's Accusations

I didn't need to watch *The Exorcist* or *The Omen* to know there is a devil loose on our planet. He's all over the news. He is made light of—carries a pitchfork and has a pointed tail and horns—but he is real, he is evil, and he does tempt and harass. And he is mentioned many times in scripture. But it wasn't until the last book of the Bible was written, almost four thousand years after our planet began, that we discover the shady context of his existence, the issues, and the war.

This war did not transpire on the outer edges of the galaxy in some uncharted solar system that only Captain Kirk, Spock, or Yoda can get to. It wasn't with a group of evolving primates with substandard IQs. Rather, it started at the control center of the universe with brilliant beings. Satan and the millions of angels who sided with him fought over important issues. Evidently, they lost the physical battle and were kicked out of heaven, but the war is still raging. What did they fight for; what were the issues? Does the Bible tell us more about why Satan rebelled?

> How you have fallen from heaven, O morning star [Lucifer], son of the dawn! You have been cast down to the earth, you who once laid low the nations! You said in your heart, "I will ascend to heaven; I will raise my throne above the stars of God; I will sit enthroned on

the mount of assembly, on the utmost heights of the sacred mountain. I will ascend above the tops of the clouds; I will make myself like the Most High." (Isa. 14:12–14)

You were the model of perfection, full of wisdom and perfect in beauty. You were in Eden, the garden of God; every precious stone adorned you: ruby, topaz and emerald, chrysolite, onyx and jasper, sapphire, turquoise and beryl. Your settings and mountings were made of gold; on the day you were created they were prepared. You were anointed as a guardian cherub, for so I ordained you. You were on the holy mount of God; you walked among the fiery stones. You were blameless in your ways from the day you were created till wickedness was found in you. Through your widespread trade you were filled with violence, and you sinned. So I drove you in disgrace from the mount of God, and I expelled you, O guardian cherub, from among the fiery stones. Your heart became proud on account of your beauty, and you corrupted your wisdom because of your splendor. (Ezek. 28:12–18)

Then he showed me Joshua the high priest standing before the angel of the LORD, and Satan standing at his right side to accuse him. The LORD said to Satan, "The Lord rebuke you, Satan! The Lord, who has chosen Jerusalem, rebuke you! Is not this man a burning stick snatched from the fire?" (Zech. 3:1–2)

One day the angels came to present themselves before the Lord, and Satan also came with them. The Lord said to Satan, "Where have you come from?" Satan answered the Lord, "From roaming through the earth and going back and forth in it." Then the Lord said to Satan, "Have you considered my servant Job? There is no one on earth like him; he is blameless and upright, a man who fears God and shuns evil." "Does Job fear God for nothing?" Satan replied. "Have you not put a hedge around him and his household and everything he has? You have blessed the work of his hands, so that his flocks and herds are spread throughout the land. But stretch out your hand and strike everything he has, and he will surely curse you to your face." The Lord said to Satan, "Very well, then, everything he has is in your hands, but on the man himself do not lay a finger." (Job 1:6–12)

These texts suggest that Satan was once an exalted angel—one of the covering cherubs overlooking the Ark of the Covenant—but fallen, beautiful but proud, intelligent but arrogant, greedy for power, even God's power, and now he is the accuser of both God and man. Notice how Satan accused Joshua of sin, and God was there to defend him. Notice too, how Satan accused God of playing favorites with Job. No wonder Revelation says that Satan is the accuser.

For the accuser of our brothers and sisters, who accuses them before our God day and night, has been hurled down … Therefore rejoice, you heavens and you who dwell in them! But woe to the earth and the sea, because the devil has gone down to you! He is filled with fury, because he knows that his time is short." (Rev. 12:10–12)

And notice that God himself is on trial. Paul wrote in Romans:

Certainly not! Indeed, let God be true but every man a liar. As it is written: "That You may be justified in Your words, and may overcome when You are judged. (Rom. 3:4, NKJV)

Is it even conceivable that God could be on trial? How or why would God need to justify His words and actions, and how could anyone take God to court? Satan must have leveled some very, very serious accusations against God and His government. And God must have laid out His case voluntarily. You can't make God do anything against His will. But as with Watergate, once the accusations start to fly, the only way to prove your innocence is with evidence. Claims carry no weight at all. In fact, anytime a man or woman, president, CEO, or even the Almighty is accused of lying, nothing they can say from that point on will change public opinion. Only by demonstrating the truth over and over and in many and various ways can a person's credibility be reestablished. God had to show the universe the truth and what He was like, and that is why He created our planet.

You can read the entire creation account in Genesis chapters 1–3, but I'll shorten it a little here to save space.

> In the beginning God created the heavens and the earth. The earth was formless and void, and darkness was over the surface of the deep, and the Spirit of God was moving over the surface of the waters.
>
> Then God said, "Let there be light"; and there was light. God saw that the light was good; ... God called the light day, and the darkness He called night. And there was evening and there was morning, one day.
>
> Then God said, "Let there be an expanse in the midst of the waters, and let it separate the waters from the waters." ... And there was evening and there was morning, a second day.
>
> Then God said, "Let the waters below the heavens be gathered into one place, and let the dry land appear"; and it was so. ... and God saw that it was good. ... There was evening and there was morning, a third day.
>
> Then God said, "Let there be lights in the expanse of the heavens to separate the day from the night ... and

God saw that it was good. There was evening and there was morning, a fourth day.

Then God said, "Let the waters teem with swarms of living creatures, and let birds fly above the earth in the open expanse of the heavens." ... and God saw that it was good. ... There was evening and there was morning, a fifth day.

Then God said, "Let the earth bring forth living creatures after their kind: cattle and creeping things and beasts of the earth after their kind"; ... and God saw that it was good.

Then God said, "Let Us make man in Our image, according to Our likeness; and let them rule over the fish of the sea and over the birds of the sky and over the cattle and over all the earth, and over every creeping thing that creeps on the earth." God created man in His own image, in the image of God He created him; male and female He created them. God blessed them; and God said to them, "Be fruitful and multiply, and fill the earth, and subdue it; and rule over the fish of the sea and over the birds of the sky and over every living thing that moves on the earth." ... God saw all that He had made, and behold, it was very good. And there was evening and there was morning, the sixth day. (Gen. chapter 1, NASV)

Thus the heavens and the earth were completed, and all their hosts. By the seventh day God completed His work which He had done, and He rested on the seventh day from all His work which He had done. ...

The Lord God planted a garden toward the east, in Eden; and there He placed the man whom He had formed. Out of the ground the Lord God caused to grow every tree that is pleasing to the sight and good for food; the tree of life also in the midst of the garden, and the tree of the knowledge of good and evil.

Then the Lord God took the man and put him into the garden of Eden to cultivate it and keep it. The Lord God commanded the man, saying, "From any tree of the garden you may eat freely; but from the tree of the knowledge of good and evil you shall not eat, *for in the day that you eat from it you will surely die*." (Gen. 2:1–2, 15–17, NASV)

Unfortunately, the story takes a twist.

Now the serpent was more crafty than any beast of the field which the Lord God had made. And he said to the woman, "Indeed, has God said, 'You shall not eat from any tree of the garden'?" The woman said to the serpent, "From the fruit of the trees of the garden we may eat; but from the fruit of the tree which is in the middle of the garden, God has said, 'You shall not eat from it or touch it, or you will die.'" The serpent said to the woman, "*You surely will not die!* For God knows that in the day you eat from it your eyes will be opened, and you will be like God, knowing good and evil." When the woman saw that the tree was good for food, and that it was a delight to the eyes, and that the tree was desirable to make one wise, she took from its fruit and ate. (Gen. 3:1–5)

In this short dialogue we see two competing statements. God said something was true, and Satan countered through the serpent. God informed Adam and Eve of the inevitable results of sinning—you will die—and Satan said it wasn't true. Eve was on the hot seat, needing to choose who to believe and who not to believe. And sadly, she sided with Satan. Eve listened to the serpent's explanation and decided to chance it.

Satan hinted that God was holding out on them by withholding this "special" fruit. He made it appear that by trusting him she would gain a greater good than by following God's direct council, and he insisted that God's comment about sin was not true.

Eve then gave the fruit to Adam, who really knew better, but wanted to be loyal to his wife. Adam knew that the serpent was really the enemy they had been warned about, and now she would be lost. But Eve was the most precious thing in his life. How could he live without her? She was a part of him, "bone of my bone and flesh of my flesh." After all, he thought, maybe the serpent is right, and we can be more; but if not, maybe God will forgive us just this one time.

Unfortunately, Adam and Eve's decision to eat the forbidden fruit was more than just disobedience; it was rebellion. And it was personally damaging. The stakes were high, and they let God down. They spurned God's love and showed their lack of honor, respect, and loyalty. It demonstrated their lack of faith. It showed their indifference toward truth and their Father's wisdom. In short, they rejected their Dad. God had already shown them his love and concern, and they scorned it. They chose Satan's side in the battle thinking that God could lie to them and withhold something good. Although they did so ignorantly, as judge and jury, they sided with Satan in the war.

After Adam and Eve sinned, God comes back into the picture.

> They heard the sound of the Lord God walking in the garden in the cool of the day, and the man and his wife hid themselves from the presence of the Lord God among the trees of the garden.

> Then the Lord God called to the man, and said to him, "Where are you?" He said, "I heard the sound of You in the garden, and I was afraid because I was naked; so I hid myself." And He said, "Who told you that you were naked? Have you eaten from the tree of which I commanded you not to eat?" The man said, "The woman whom You gave *to be* with me, she gave me from

the tree, and I ate." Then the Lord God said to the woman, "What is this you have done?" And the woman said, "The serpent deceived me, and I ate."

The Lord God said to the serpent, "Because you have done this, cursed are you more than all cattle, and more than every beast of the field; on your belly you will go, and dust you will eat all the days of your life. To the woman He said, "I will greatly multiply your pain in childbirth, in pain you will bring forth children; yet your desire will be for your husband, and he will rule over you." To Adam he said, "Because you listened to your wife and ate fruit from the tree about which I commanded you, 'You must not eat from it'; cursed is the ground because of you; In toil you will eat of it all the days of your life. Both thorns and thistles it shall grow for you; and you will eat the plants of the field; by the sweat of your face you will eat bread, till you return to the ground, because from it you were taken; for you are dust, and to dust you shall return." ...

Then the Lord God said, "Behold, the man has become like one of Us, knowing good and evil; and now, he might stretch out his hand, and take also from the tree of life, and eat, and live forever. So He drove the man out; and at the east of the garden of Eden He stationed the cherubim and the flaming sword which turned every direction to guard the way to the tree of life. (Gen. 3:8–24)

We can't hear the tone of God's voice or see the look on His face, but it seems as if God is angry. He tells the serpent he will live out his life crawling on his belly. He tells Adam He is going to curse the ground and make his work harder. He tells Eve she is going to have pain in childbearing and will need to submit to her husband. He tells both of them they will be barred from eating from the Tree of Life and someday die: "dust thou art, and dust thou shall become." God even repeats the serpent's claim that Adam and Eve "would be like God, knowing good and evil." What an amazing turn of events. What starts out sublime, ends in disaster.

Imagine if you can, floating in space just above our planet, knowing what has already happened in heaven. You also know Lucifer personally. He has come to your planet many times to bring new ideas to your civilization. He has helped engineer your planet's greatest structures and led your grandest symphonies. He is renowned for his brilliance and power and glory. His presence is formidable. He's dazzling. Compared to you he might as well be a god, the difference is so stark. And he has never said anything negative about God before. On the contrary, Lucifer has always been one of God's greatest supporters. But now you hear of this controversy. Lucifer has accused God of holding His creatures back and of lying. How could that be true? Why would God lie? Why would Lucifer lie? He had never said or done anything to excite your suspicion before. And now you have witnessed the creation of planet Earth, listened in on what Lucifer told Eve, and now you are seeing God punish Adam and Eve. Many things have been said, and demonstrated, on both sides. What is the truth? What are the issues? What are we looking for in these stories?

Let's go very slowly and look at these events from an outsider's perspective, and try to put the puzzle together.

First, it seems as though God thinks Lucifer is too proud and wants too much power, control, and fame. Lucifer, on the other hand, thinks God is too controlling, is holding His creatures back from success, and is selfishly withholding His creative power and authority.

And second, God said if you sin and go against His will, you will die. Satan claims that sin doesn't cause death.

Can you imagine seeing God and Lucifer arguing, toe to toe, saying these things in public, in the hearing of all those in heaven? These are just the first sparks to fly, and you can bet there will be more. What does the evidence tell us so far? Is God really too restrictive? Is Lucifer really too puffed up? What do you think? Do we have enough information to decide?

The creation was impressive, and God gave Adam and Eve a lot of power and freedom, but God's restriction to not eat the fruit seems a little petty, and to die for eating the wrong fruit one time, seems extreme. On the other hand, Lucifer has not shown us much of his character except he used a serpent to disguise himself when he talked to Eve. Maybe we should wait awhile before we decide.

What about the second question? God said the day you sin you will die, and Adam and Eve did not die. Moreover, Satan has sinned many times, and he is still alive. It looks like Lucifer has a point. He could be right with issue number two. If it is true that sin does not cause death, then God was not telling the truth, or at least we don't understand what God meant by what He said. It could be that this rule God gave was actually just a threat designed to keep Adam and Eve from going against His will. It could also mean that you will die someday, but then we would still have to ask: how would you die, and why? It looks like Lucifer may have the upper hand at the moment with issue number two.

If Lucifer is correct, then there is a word to describe God's rule: arbitrary. Many people only vaguely understand the term, so let me give you some examples. Nonarbitrary laws or rules have specific natural consequences, such as jumping off the Grand Canyon without a parachute: you will, under gravity's attraction, strike the bottom with great force and probably die. Drinking gasoline, standing in front of speeding trains, or driving a stake into your eye, all of these have natural, nonarbitrary consequences. On the other hand, most of the laws in our land, even our good laws, often have arbitrary consequences. Take stealing, for example. If you rip off a car in California, you can be charged under a misdemeanor or a felony, and depending on circumstances, you can be fined up to $5,000 and serve up to three years in jail. It is not that the consequences don't fit the crime, but there is an arbitrary sliding scale. If you steal the same car in Texas, you could do between five and ninety-nine years in jail, depending on how much the car was worth, and pay up to $10,000 in fines. It is not that one state has better laws than the other; it is just that the penalty is a moving target; it is changeable—it is arbitrary. I found that some laws are not arbitrary at all. After having a back operation, the doctor told me not to lift anything more than ten to fifteen pounds, but did I listen? I lifted a thirty- to forty-pound bike (one wheel at a time and for only about ten seconds), but I ruined my back and the surgery, suffered for months with sciatic lightning strikes burning down my legs and into my feet, and needed a second surgery. The doctor's fifteen-pound rule was not arbitrary; he was just stating facts, not imposing a penalty.

Since Adam and Eve didn't immediately die, it appears as though God's death penalty is imposed, thus—arbitrary. Why wasn't the penalty no fruit from the Tree of Life for two weeks or a weeklong time-out outside the garden? Evidently, if you eat the wrong fruit, the imposed penalty is death.

Assuming for a while that God's death penalty is imposed, what does it imply? First, it suggests that God is the type of person who could give arbitrary rules. That does not speak very well of our heavenly Father. It suggests He needs to control people with threats and not with reason. It also suggests that God is exacting in His requests. And, unfortunately, the situation only gets worse. After they go against His will, God punishes them severely, and for their first-ever mistake. They were kicked out of the garden and made to work hard to provide food for themselves outside the verdant garden. Eve was to have pain multiplied in childbirth and submit to Adam. And eventually, the two were to die, because God would withhold the life-giving fruit from the Tree of Life. At the end of the day, Lucifer could add to his accusations that God is arbitrary, exacting, unforgiving, severe, and a liar about sin causing death, and is not someone you can trust. What a list!

CHAPTER 3

How Can You Trust a God as Described?

This appears to be the gist of the accusations raised by Lucifer. How could anyone, angels or man, trust God if He were as Satan claims? Without more evidence, who in their right mind would want to place their life in His hands? There must be strong evidence, proven over and over and under many and varied circumstances, to change the tide of public opinion. But where can we get more evidence? Where can we go to get an unbiased, truthful explanation? The Bible. And that is why it is so thick. If all God wanted was obedient servants He could have made the Bible about twenty pages and listed all the rules with their appropriate punishments, but the Bible isn't just a list of does and don'ts; it is the true history of the war, and how God is involved. The Bible is the record, and God wants us to understand the evidence.

The Bible has been studied by the world's greatest scholars; it has been analyzed letter by letter and has been judged as the greatest collection of literature in the world. Both in style and content, the Bible is in a class by itself. I could tell you of the world's greatest scientists and leaders who believe it. I could tell you of its matchless preservation and internal consistency and of the massive amount of archeological data that supports its history, but only reading it for yourself will convince you that the book is what it claims to be—the word of God.

Just consider some of the great men and women of history who have believed and loved the scriptures. The musicians J. S. Bach, Handel, and Fanny Crosby dedicated their lives and music to God's cause. Writers T. S. Eliot, C. S. Lewis, E. G. White, and Dorothy Sayers wrote thousands of pages. Catherine and William Booth started the Salvation Army. Artists Rembrandt and Da Vinci; preachers Billy Graham, Dwight Moody, Martin Luther, and Martin Luther King Jr.; and scientists Newton, Kepler, Boyle, Kelvin, Ray, Pasteur, Faraday, Maxwell, Bacon, Galileo, Descartes, Steno, Mendel, Carver, and Planck bucked the establishment and chose to serve God rather than man. These are just a few of the billions of people who have trusted the Bible. Though it is not always a popular book, I would love to add my name to the list of those who believe and trust the Bible.

Yet, even though the Bible itself is true, how people interpret the many stories may not be. Some people have muddied the water by not reading the whole book, taking snippets here and there, and forgetting all the rest. Some only accept the New Testament as inspired and miss a great deal. And as discussed before, many people have not considered the war in enough detail. But this is wrong. Without the war, the context is incomplete.

So in the following pages I would like to take another look at the Bible and God's actions, in a broader, Great Controversy setting.

CHAPTER 4

Great Controversy Perspective

Let's backtrack a little so we can take a look at the creation from a different angle. After Lucifer's initial accusations and after the angelic host took sides, God created our world.

The orderly creation of our planet was not for us. We didn't show up until day six; we were not there to watch it unfold, but the angels and other worlds were. In six dramatic days, God created our planet—slowly, deliberately, majestically—and made mankind to rule it. He could have formed it all in an instant, but He didn't; it is as if He were creating a sonata one note at a time just to increase the suspense. At the end of each matchless day, God said humbly that it was good. I'm sure those looking on had a lot to talk about—a spectacular planet was rolling off God's fingertips, and in slow motion.

What had He done? Look at the magnificent blue marble floating in space, spinning. There are myriads of colorful plants and furry animals scattered across Earth's vastness, all with the ability to procreate life. Behold Eve's beauty, Adam's strength, and the intelligence He gave this staggering pair. He made plans for Adam and Eve to complete the creation of the world with little ones born in their own image, and then rule everything on Earth as His personal representatives. God did not skimp when endowing our planet and first parents.

21

After the six days of creation, God invited Adam and Eve and all those looking on to stop, rest, and consider His creation. The seventh day was given as a memorial of God's creative power and the beginning of His answers to the questions that had been riveting heaven. It gave everyone time to consider what God had just done and measure its significance.

With the war still fresh in your mind, can you think of any charges God may have attempted to answer during creation week? How about, is God selfish with His creative power, or is God a controlling dictator or micromanager? Consider the gifts He shared with Adam and Eve—making little ones in their own image. We don't know all that is necessary to bring forth life, but we do get to help create it. And God made Adam and Eve king and queen of the planet; they were the "gods" of Earth. God gave them, and us, incredible powers and freedom.

CHAPTER 5

The Answer Gets Blurred

Next, we see a beautiful garden and two special trees, the Tree of Life and the tree of the Knowledge of Good and Evil. We see God confine Satan to the tree of Good and Evil, and warn the innocent pair to stay away. God would not allow Satan the freedom to pick the time and place to tempt Adam and Eve, tempting them beyond their ability to resist. God really does value nothing higher than preserving our freedom of choice, and at this point in time, they were no match for Satan's cunning and brilliance. With this arrangement, God could protect Adam and Eve and still allow Satan an open forum to voice his arguments against Himself; that is, if they wanted to listen, but it would be Adam and Eve's choice to confront him and not the other way around.

Then God ordered Adam and Eve to not eat the fruit. Why, was the fruit bad? No. God knew that Satan would lie to them, just like he lied to the angels, in an attempt to trick them into joining his rebellion, and there needed to be a clear indicator as to their decision. So the fruit was really *symbolic*, like baptism is symbolic. Baptism is an outward expression of an inward change or a decision. The picking and eating of the fruit signified the decision: trust God and leave it alone; trust Satan and eat the fruit. Like a litmus test, it was easy to see which side they were on.

Next, Eve leaves Adam behind and wanders over to the tree by accident. While gazing at the tree, she is alerted to the serpent's presence and converses with him. She listens and swallows his lies—hook, line, and sinker—that God is selfish, not wanting competition from some other "superior being," which is what Eve would be if she ate the special fruit, and that God could lie about the results of sin—all in one short conversation. After weighing the two sides, Eve chose to believe a snake instead of her loving Father, and she eats the fruit. Soon after, Adam eats the fruit too, making his decision to stand with Eve. Then they discover that sin is real and not merely something recorded in a book. Sin has real consequences: they lost their covering of light; they saw their shame; they felt naked; fear replaced their love for God, and they ran and hid in the garden. They no longer saw God as friendly. They were afraid because they had bought the ugly lie that God was not friendly and should be feared.

We are left in a perplexing situation. Heaven has been ripped apart by a proverbial bomb blast of accusations and is hemorrhaging. Then God tries to stop the bleeding by creating our world and Adam and Eve, only to have them trade sides. The patient is going from bad to worse. Heaven is in crisis!

What is God going to do? What are His options? He could wipe out our memories, and no one would ever be the wiser. Anytime a person or angel had a bad thought He could erase it, but God does not want to be the heavenly Big Brother or thought police. He could destroy the evidence—the Earth and Adam and Eve—and start over. But what would Satan say, except that God had failed and that he was right in his accusations. Or, God could wipe out everyone and everything, including Satan and the angels, and start over. But what would the rest of the universe say? Would they cry foul? Would that be fair to God's loyal followers? No, and rebellion would spread. What if God were to destroy every living being: men, women, good and bad angels, and all the other beings on all the other planets and start over? If He did, then we would never know how many times God has had to try and try again to get it right. It would also suggest His ways were not perfect and that Satan was right. Again, not a very satisfying picture of our Heavenly Father.

There is one more possibility. God could go the full distance and prove Himself true, righteous, and holy regardless of the accusations, regardless of how badly we behave, and regardless of the personal cost to Himself. He could demonstrate the truth that Satan is wrong, that sin does kill all by itself, and that He is loving and friendly and not arbitrary, exacting, unforgiving, and severe. He did it and called it the Plan of Salvation.

CHAPTER 6

God Hints at the Plan of Salvation—the Gospel

M any people attempt to explain the Plan of Salvation in short, ten-second sound bites, such as: Jesus died for you, or just believe and be saved. But as you can see by the issue's complexity, the remedy is not going to be easy or cheap; the answers will be at least as complicated as the issues. Our generation always seeks instant answers to complex problems that defy easy solutions. Easy answers, short sound bites, and proof texts are just not going to happen.

God begins to explain the Plan of Salvation when He speaks to the serpent.

> And I will put enmity between you and the woman, and between your offspring and hers; he will crush your head, and you will strike his heel." (Gen. 3:15)

In cryptic language, God gives us a promise. I will put enmity or hostility between you (Satan) and mankind, and you will be destroyed even though you cripple the race. In essence, God is promising more pain and suffering and strife and death for our planet, but eventually a victory. It is as if God said, "Okay, Satan, you won round one, but the fight is just getting started, and I know how it ends!"

How else can we describe what God has promised—this good news? Traditionally it is said that Adam and Eve sinned and deserved to die because of their disobedience, and God would make a way of escape. But this is too simplistic. Their sin was not merely disobeying some rule; it was not breaking some crystal vase that can be glued back together again; it was not just taking a few Oreo cookies that can be given back. Rather, their sin was multifaceted and relational, and it is in the past. What can you do with words or attitudes that happened yesterday? I've seen people eat their words, but you can't really take them back. They hurt. They do real damage. For Adam and Eve, it was a change in their attitude toward God. They believed Satan's lie that God could lie and is not trustworthy. No, He's scary—like Charles Manson or Ted Bundy is scary. The ramifications of their new belief, their "sin", are vast. But greater than their tragedy are the ones still surrounding God and His policies. The big issues have not changed. Adam and Eve just muddied the water.

For ages, men, women, and churches have tried to fix sin, and they usually focus on a person's behavior and utilize behavior modification principles; they focus on sin as being just disobedience and breaking commandments and stress that we just need to try harder to resist temptation. But sin isn't just an action; it begins in the mind with a corrupt concept of what God is like, and that is where you have to start. First correct our distorted image of God. Any other mechanism is worthless. God's only method to heal and save is to present truth to the mind: "the truth will set you free" (John 8:23). He does not use force, coercion, magic, intimidation, or any other shortcut to healing.

How do you fix relational sin? Evidence. And that is what the rest of the Bible is about, and the gospel, and the plan of salvation; it is all light, truth, and evidence regarding God's real character. God did not just make claims. He is going to show us, and the universe, what He is like and answer the accusations that have been leveled against Him.

Paul knew what the gospel was.

For I am not ashamed of the *gospel*; it is the power of God for salvation to everyone who has faith, to the Jew first and also to the Greek. For in it the *righteousness of God is revealed* through faith for faith; as it is written, "The one who is righteous will live by faith." (Rom. 1:16–17, NRSV)

And so did Jeremiah.

This is what the Lord says: "Let not the wise man boast of his wisdom or the strong man boast of his strength or the rich man boast of his riches, but let him who boasts boast about this: that he understands and knows me, that *I am the Lord, who exercises kindness, justice and righteousness on earth, for in these I delight*," declares the Lord. (Jer. 9:23–24)

The good news—the gospel—is really just knowing the truth about God, and Adam and Eve, you and I, and the rest of the universe have a lot to learn. Jesus said:

Now this is eternal life: that they know you, the only true God, and Jesus Christ, whom you have sent. (John 17:3)

Sin, lying, deceit, death—all these things are new to God's universe. No one understood these things at first; no one had any experience with greedy salesmen, corrupt politicians, or phony religious leaders, and no one had ever seen something die. God has had to work really hard to educate His creatures regarding the consequences, but He couldn't let them experience all of the consequences—they would die.

Early on, when Satan did not get his way and rebelled, I'm sure God explained to him that if he persisted in his unfounded self-exaltation he would die—just like He explained the facts to Adam and Eve in the garden. But no one—no one at all—really knew what death looked like. They had never seen a tulip wilt in the heat, much less a murder or the true consequences of sin. I'm sure Satan got the message that he was not going to be living any longer, but wondered, would this event be fast or slow? Would it take decades, like cancer? Was it die for a day and come back tomorrow? Was it the result of some natural cause, or was it imposed? And who was going to do it? Was God going to kill him personally with a knife or lightning bolt, or was He going to have the "good" angels kill for Him?

Satan might have said, "Die? You are just going to kill me! There is nothing natural about this! God, when You're challenged, You cover up the truth with threats of death to protect Your arbitrary control. What You really mean, but won't say, is: You will kill me if I don't obey!"

In truth, God has had to supernaturally keep some of sin's effects from occurring. He said sin kills, and it does, but it is so horrid that God didn't want any of His children to experience it without giving everyone the chance to see what He meant first, and He'll show us this later. He had another reason too. Had He allowed sin to kill Satan after Satan had accused Him of wrongdoing, it would look like God killed him in retaliation or as a cover-up. This would scare the angels and fear would poison everyone, destroying every shred of trust they had in God. God had to preserve Satan and the others because it was the only way the universe could see the truth.

After the rebellion of Adam and Eve, God had to deal with problems on two fronts. Now He has Satan's accusations to deal with, and needs to keep Adam and Eve and their progeny from going over the cliff. It is time God takes action. There isn't any more God can do for Satan; he has already made up his mind to rebel, but Adam and Eve have more to learn. So God sets out to discipline His children, *but discipline can be misunderstood.*

Adam and Eve were removed from their perfect garden home to better learn the necessary lessons of life. Outside the garden, they saw what sin was like through a changed nature; they saw death and disease as the results of rebellion, and the beautiful garden would remind them of what God had offered and what they had lost. It may look harsh from the sidelines, but Adam and Eve needed work to occupy their minds as a safeguard. Habits of self-control, diligence, and sacrifice could not be gained in their old home because of their new, selfish, sinful condition. God was not punishing them, but with their recent demise, they would be even weaker than before and even less able to resist Satan's temptations. They needed God's help.

CHAPTER 7

Cain to the Flood

Quickly, the climate became harsh; the earth yielded its noxious weeds, and in no time, Eve bore two sons, Cain and Abel. Like many families today, the boys were opposites: Abel kept the flocks, and Cain tilled the ground. They were opposites in character too. Out of jealousy, Cain slew his righteous brother Abel while out in the field. It didn't take very long for sin to degrade the race, moving from good to bad in one generation.

This is the first recorded death in the Bible. Does this help explain what God meant when He said if you sin you will die? Did He mean that we will turn on each other like wolves? Our planet has become a violent place with almost half a million homicides every year. As bad as it seems in the United States, with about thirteen thousand murders a year, several countries have rates more than ten times higher. Nothing more is said about death in this first case of domestic violence. I guess we'll just keep looking for clues.

After this first murder, God did not invoke the death penalty but stepped in and put a special mark on Cain so no one would hurt this earthly parallel to Satan. This way the universe could begin to see the results of sin in people—and what happened next? Genesis 6:5 says "the wickedness of the earth was great," so much so that God was sorry He had created mankind. "It grieved His heart." The people were corrupted by Cain's sinful influence.

What did the angels and unfallen worlds learn from Cain's example and evil influence? It would have been best if Cain's career had been terminated immediately after killing Abel, and God should have let the natural consequences of sin fall on Satan as soon as he passed the point of no return. Then the other angels, and all of us, would not be ruined by his groundless accusations and evil influence. But again, since no one in the universe had ever seen sin and its results, no one would have understood their deaths. It would have been assumed that God had killed His adversaries, and that would have created an intense fear of God in all His creatures.

CHAPTER 8

The Flood—What Happens If You Fear God?

"So how do we get rid of sin now?" the loyal angels may have asked. The Earth is populated with sinful, selfish, cruel, evil beings. Maybe God asked for suggestions—we don't know. What we do know is, He sent a message of hope to all who wanted to be saved (Gen. 6:3). For 120 years Noah preached to the world, but to no avail. All the antediluvians needed to do was trust God and his representative, Noah, enough to get on a boat. God is always willing to rescue, heal, and save, but the people refused His offer. Only eight people entered the Ark, and then God destroyed the world in a terrifying display of might and power. The destruction was so complete that geologists are still trying to unravel the sedimentary mess.

God could have destroyed those wicked people in an infinite number of ways. He could have put them to sleep, given them all heart attacks, made them all vanish, or killed them with some quick and merciful disease. But He chose not to do any of those things because He needed to demonstrate something else: Did the destruction of sin and evil with massive amounts of power win God any friends? Did wiping out sin in a powerful manifestation prevent sin after the world's destruction? God saved eight. They were the best on the planet. But after the flood, and after the planet repopulated some, the people built the tower of Babel to escape Him (Gen. 11:4). God made a promise to Noah that He wouldn't destroy the world again with a flood (Gen. 9:8–17), but the people didn't believe He would honor His promise. It wasn't that they didn't believe in God. No, now they believed, and trembled. God demonstrated to the universe that you can't get rid of sin and rebellion with power or force; but rather, unrestrained power produces fear, and fear destroys love and produces rebellion. Even when it is used for good, might and power can produce a disastrous harvest.

This has several applications. How often do parents, employers, unions, and nations resort to power and force? Not that there isn't an appropriate time for such, but it is certainly plagued with negative consequences. Might and power may seem to get things done quickly, but if it leaves men, women, nations, or our children cowering, they will not respect you, much less love you, and they will rebel, and if given a chance—retaliate.

With respect to the future, consider God's ultimate power in the judgment. Talk about having power over someone! God's power to save or destroy is unparalleled and could be terrifying if misused or misunderstood. We'll pick this up again later, but, obviously, if God were to attempt to crush out sin on judgment day and leave those still standing in fear, the results would be similar: sin would not be destroyed; it would be tilled, watered, and fertilized.

This is the second description of death. Is this God's answer to the question, if you sin you will die? Many think so. Let's keep looking for clues.

If might and power won't work, how do you get rid of fear and rebellion? You could start by making and keeping promises, and by demonstrating that you are trustworthy and can be depended upon. You might start with a covenant.

CHAPTER 9

The Covenants

Call of Abraham

After the flood and subsequent destruction of the Tower of Babel, God calls Abram, later called Abraham, to continue the saga. Abram grew up in Ur, Mesopotamia, a large city for its day, situated next to the Euphrates River. Today we'd say he lived near Nasiriyah, in southern Iraq. Abram; his wife, Sarai; his father, Terah; and his nephew, Lot, left Ur and started toward Canaan, but they stopped short in Harran. Terah dies in Harran, and that is where God called Abram from. At seventy-five, Abram left his home, his companions, and the comforts of city life, and took Sarai, Lot, and all his possessions over one hundred miles to Canaan, on foot, just because God asked.

> The Lord had said to Abram, "Go from your country, your people and your father's household to the land I will show you. I will make you into a great nation, and I will bless you; I will make your name great, and you will be a blessing. I will bless those who bless you, and whoever curses you I will curse; and all peoples on earth will be blessed through you." (Gen. 12:1–3)

37

Two great nations did come from Abram's loins—the Arab nations via Ishmael and Israel through Isaac. And God did bless Abraham with flocks and herds, power and influence, and family. Abraham was blessed over and again and commended for his righteousness. No less than three times (Rom. 4:3; Gal. 3:6; James 2:23) do New Testament writers remind us that Abraham's faith is what God is looking for in His people:

> Abram believed the Lord, and he credited it to him as righteousness. He also said to him, "I am the Lord, who brought you out of Ur of the Chaldeans to give you this land to take possession of it."

> But Abram said, "Sovereign Lord, how can I know that I will gain possession of it?"

> So the Lord said to him, "Bring me a heifer, a goat and a ram, each three years old, along with a dove and a young pigeon."

> Abram brought all these to him, cut them in two and arranged the halves opposite each other; the birds, however, he did not cut in half. Then birds of prey came down on the carcasses, but Abram drove them away. As the sun was setting, Abram fell into a deep sleep, and a thick and dreadful darkness came over him. Then the Lord said to him, "Know for certain that for four hundred years your descendants will be strangers in a country not their own and that they will be enslaved and mistreated there. But I will punish the nation they serve as slaves, and afterward they will come out with great possessions. You, however, will go to your ancestors in peace and be buried at a good old age. In the fourth generation your descendants will come back here, for the sin of the Amorites has not yet reached its full measure."

When the sun had set and darkness had fallen, a smoking firepot with a blazing torch appeared and passed between the pieces. On that day the Lord made a covenant with Abram and said, "To your descendants I give this land, from the Wadi of Egypt to the great river, the Euphrates—the land of the Kenites, Kenizzites, Kadmonites, Hittites, Perizzites, Rephaites, Amorites, Canaanites, Girgashites and Jebusites." (Gen. 15:6–21)

In this covenant, both parties were supposed to go through the Berith ceremony (Roth, 2000), a ceremony where animals were sacrificed, split in two from top to bottom (unless they were birds) and placed in two parallel lines, lines about five feet from each other, and spaced just wide enough so the two making the covenant could walk between them and make their promise of solidarity. The dead animals were symbolic, representing what would happen to a participant if he/she were to fail to uphold his or her end of the agreement or bargain. However, Abram was exhausted after waiting and protecting the animals all day from scavengers, and he slept. He did not join in. God was the only one to participate; God was the only one to walk between the animals and make the promise, which is significant. It was a one-sided promise. God would do everything. He, not we, would keep the promise. God promised that Abram's descendants would have the land.

CHAPTER 10

Abraham's Life and
Called a Friend

Abram's life is exemplary. He rescues his nephew Lot when Lot is taken captive by King Kedorlaomer. He helps illustrate what God would do one day when he offers Isaac as a sacrifice, and he pleads for the people in Sodom and Gomorrah when God tells him He is going to destroy it.

> Then the Lord said, "Shall I hide from Abraham what I am about to do? Abraham will surely become a great and powerful nation, and all nations on earth will be blessed through him. For I have chosen him, so that he will direct his children and his household after him to keep the way of the LORD by doing what is right and just, so that the LORD will bring about for Abraham what he has promised him."

> Then the Lord said, "The outcry against Sodom and Gomorrah is so great and their sin so grievous that I will go down and see if what they have done is as bad as the outcry that has reached me. If not, I will know."

The men turned away and went toward Sodom, but
Abraham remained standing before the Lord. Then
Abraham approached him and said: "Will you sweep
away the righteous with the wicked? What if there are
fifty righteous people in the city? Will you really sweep
it away and not spare the place for the sake of the fifty
righteous people in it? Far be it from you to do such a
thing—to kill the righteous with the wicked, treating
the righteous and the wicked alike. Far be it from you!
Will not the Judge of all the earth do right?"

The Lord said, "If I find fifty righteous people in the city
of Sodom, I will spare the whole place for their sake."

Then Abraham spoke up again: "Now that I have been
so bold as to speak to the Lord, though I am nothing
but dust and ashes, what if the number of the righteous
is five less than fifty? Will you destroy the whole city for
lack of five people?"

"If I find forty-five there," he said, "I will not destroy it."

Once again he spoke to him, "What if only forty are
found there?"
He said, "For the sake of forty, I will not do it."

Then he said, "May the Lord not be angry, but let me
speak. What if only thirty can be found there?"
He answered, "I will not do it if I find thirty there."

Abraham said, "Now that I have been so bold as to speak
to the Lord, what if only twenty can be found there?"
He said, "For the sake of twenty, I will not destroy it."

Then he said, "May the Lord not be angry, but let me
speak just once more. What if only ten can be found
there?"

He answered, "For the sake of ten, I will not destroy it."

When the Lord had finished speaking with Abraham, he left, and Abraham returned home. (Gen. 18:17–33)

Abraham tells the Creator of the universe, "Shouldn't the God of heaven and earth do what is right?" when God tells him He is going to destroy the cities. Abraham was definitely not merely God's servant. A servant would have said, "Anything you say," and gotten out of the way, but Abraham enjoyed a different type of relationship with God. Their relationship was personal and intimate. He loved God deeply and was looking out for God's reputation. In the end, God called Abraham His friend (Isaiah 41:8, James 2:23).

There is a whole spectrum of possible relationships a person can have with God—some good and others bad, but there is one in the middle to watch out for. Some people say they love God but fear Him too. If asked why they do what they do, they may say something like, "Well, if I don't, God will roast me." This group of worshipers enjoys a servant-like relationship, which is admirable, except that Jesus Himself asked us for something better:

> I no longer call you servants, because a servant does not know his master's business. Instead, I have called you friends, for everything that I learned from my Father I have made known to you. You did not choose me, but I chose you and appointed you so that you might go and bear fruit—fruit that will last—and so that whatever you ask in my name the Father will give you. (John 15:15–17)

Friends make life rich. It is God's relationship of choice. Even married lovers are happiest when they are friends too. Friends trust each other to cover their back, to help in times of need, and to lift them up when they need encouragement. Friends are the family we get to choose. Jesus said He really does not want the relationship of a servant, but would rather we were his friends. And notice the reason for His request: a servant does not know his master's business. God wants us to understand, to ask questions, to learn. God is interested in having His children understand Him and the deep things of scripture. God detests mechanical, memorized, unthinking, ceremonial, rote types of worship and their corresponding shallow relationships.

> Then the Lord said, "Because this people draw near with their words and honor Me with their lip service, but they remove their hearts far from Me, and their reverence for Me consists of tradition learned *by rote*. (Isa. 29:13 New American Standard Version)

Sadly, however, many people settle for less than the ideal relationship, not knowing that God has better things in mind: He wants to be our best friend. However, out of fear of the judgment and distrust, people keep God at arm's length, actually preferring a servant-like relationship. This is better than being a hardened, venomous rebel, but still far short of the relationship He had with Abraham.

After Abraham pleads with God, God destroys Sodom, Gomorrah, and the nearby cities with fire anyway. Evidently, there were not ten worthy people in the district. Angels went down and escorted Lot and his family out of town, but Lot's wife wanted to stay. After being warned, she turned back toward Sodom and was crystallized. This is the third time we see death, and the second time we see it is God that does it. What are we to learn? Is this the way God always acts when His children get out of control? Is this an example of what judgment is like, or is this just an emergency measure, a time where God is keeping rebellion from spinning out of control? Let's add this to our bag of clues.

CHAPTER 11

Abraham to the Exodus

E
ven though Abraham enjoyed a special friendship with God, he wasn't perfect. In Genesis 17:1 God tells Abram, "walk before me faithfully and be blameless," and changes his name to Abraham. He also changes Sarai's name to Sarah. Evidently, Abraham was not quite living up to God's expectations, and God gave him and his descendants the rite of circumcision, which became part of the covenant. Circumcision was to be an outward sign of an inner reality, a symbol of their devotion, dedication, and determination to be God's special representatives on Earth. Circumcision, like many other rules, was added to help keep them from sinning, because they needed it. In this case, God was helping His people keep from committing both physical and spiritual adultery. The land was crawling with idol worshipers who incorporated sex with cult prostitutes into their worship services. Giving the men a visible sign, or marker identifying them with Jehovah, would help them stay true when tempted by these heathen women and false religions.

After Abraham's stellar life, we see a downward spiral in his offspring (with the notable exception of Joseph). It is not that Isaac and Jacob were spiritual losers, but they didn't rise up to Abraham's Olympic standard.

Abraham had eight sons, but the two important ones are Ishmael and Isaac. Ishmael was Abraham's first son conceived through Hagar,

Sarah's handmaid. Isaac was the son God promised, via Sarah. God made Ishmael the father of the Arab nations and gave Isaac Abraham's vast fortune and covenant blessing.

> Then God said, "Yes, but your wife Sarah will bear you a son, and you will call him Isaac. I will establish my covenant with him as an everlasting covenant for his descendants after him. And as for Ishmael, I have heard you: I will surely bless him; I will make him fruitful and will greatly increase his numbers. He will be the father of twelve rulers, and I will make him into a great nation. But my covenant I will establish with Isaac, whom Sarah will bear to you by this time next year." (Gen. 17:19–22)

When Isaac is old enough, he marries Rebecca, who has twins, Jacob and Esau. You may remember Esau is red and hairy in complexion, the first born, and heir to both the spiritual and property birthrights, but he also despised the spiritual birthright and did not want to lead the fight against evil. He sold his birthright to Jacob for a bowl of lentil soup.

Jacob then deceives his blind and dying father. He pretends to be his brother Esau in order to obtain the birthright blessings, and, ironically, after fleeing to Paddan Aram he is deceived by his father-in-law, Laban, who switches his two daughters on their wedding night. He trades the younger, beautiful Rachel, for Leah, and makes Jacob work an additional seven years on the family ranch for payment.

Jacob, then, has twelve sons, ten of which conspire to kill his favorite son—Joseph. And Joseph was a dreamer.

> Now Israel loved Joseph more than any of his other sons, because he had been born to him in his old age; and he made an ornate robe for him. When his brothers saw that their father loved him more than any of them, they hated him and could not speak a kind word to him.

Joseph had a dream, and when had told it to his brothers, they hated him all the more.

He said to them, "Listen to this dream I had: We were binding sheaves of grain out in the field when suddenly my sheaf rose and stood upright, while your sheaves gathered around mine and bowed down to it."

His brothers said to him, "Do you intend to reign over us? Will you actually rule us?" And they hated him all the more because of his dream and what he had said.

Then he had another dream, and he told it to his brothers. "Listen," he said, "I had another dream, and this time the sun and moon and eleven stars were bowing down to me." (Gen. 37:3–9)

While off tending the sheep, the ten capture him, strip off his fancy coat, and stuff him down a deep well. He begs his brothers to show him mercy, but they pull him out only to trade him like a side of beef to slave traders going to Egypt. They sell Joseph, and their souls, for twenty pieces of silver.

Joseph

Joseph is an enigma. With no recorded sins, he goes from slave to chancellor, but only after being thrown in jail after being accused of seducing the governor's wife. After interpreting two more dreams, he is brought out of the dungeon and promoted. Second only to Pharaoh, he directs the nation's affairs and prepares the Middle East for the coming disaster. For seven years Joseph stores the grain and produce of Egypt's bumper crops to be dispersed during the seven years of drought. The famine brings Joseph's brothers to Egypt, where they bow before him like their sheaves of grain once did in his dream. Through Joseph, God preserved His people from famine, but will Israel preserve Egypt?

Joseph's descendants forget God and His ways, and ultimately, the Israelites are enslaved by Egypt. For more than four hundred years they carry water, make mud bricks to build their master's cities, and clean the homes and chamber pots of their captors. Their internment lasted twice as long as the United States has been in existence. The heartless, ruthless, pitiless oppression led them to despair. But before being crushed out of existence, the Israelites cry out to the Lord.

God heard their prayers, saw their misery, and used Moses, Aaron, and ten plagues to discredit the gods of Egypt. Each of the plagues was designed to strike down one of the impotent Egyptian gods. They worshipped the sun, the Nile River, and cattle; they even worshipped flies and Pharaoh and his firstborn son. In mercy to both the ignorant Egyptians and Israelites, God showed that the things they bowed down to were worthless—that only He had the power they craved and worshiped. God came to their rescue, gave them back their freedom, and broke the bonds of their cruel captors.

CHAPTER 12

The Ten Commandments

Israelites, Egyptians, and people from many nations fled out of Egypt. They marched through the Red Sea and trudged across the desert for three months before camping around Mount Sinai. God's followers were no longer just decedents of Abraham but anyone who wanted to follow Him, including the Egyptians. God is the god of all people, and He wanted everyone to get off on the right foot, so He gave them the Ten Commandments for guidance. God called his newly liberated people to the mountain to talk, but they were afraid. Shaking in their boots and knees knocking, they pleaded with Moses to intercede for them.

> When the people saw the thunder and lightning and heard the trumpet and saw the mountain in smoke, they trembled with fear. They stayed at a distance and said to Moses, "Speak to us yourself and we will listen. But do not have God speak to us or we will die." Moses said to the people, "Do not be afraid. God has come to test you, so that the fear of God will be with you to keep you from sinning." (Exod. 20:18–20)

Moses told them they had nothing to fear. God had just miraculously saved them from the Egyptians and watched over them with a pillar of fire by night and a shady, cooling cloud by day. Of course God was not to be feared. God was only trying to get their attention, and their respect, so they would take Him and His commands seriously.

God sent lightning, earthquakes, and thunder in an attempt to instill some level of reverence (as all parents and teachers know, you won't be taken seriously without respect). And He gave them the commandments because they were barbaric. They needed to realize that lying, stealing, cheating, coveting, and adultery were wrong. It is sad to think that God had to tell His children to stop killing their brothers and sisters, but that is the type of people with which God had to work.

And God allowed them to have an intercessor, not because He is unapproachable and fearsome, or that He wanted or needed a mediator, but because Israel clamored for one. They grew up in Egypt, and intercessors were an integral part of religion. There, no one went straight to their gods—gods were to be feared and appeased.

Jesus said this about us needing an intercessor:

> Though I have been speaking figuratively, a time is coming when I will no longer use this kind of language but will tell you plainly about my Father. In that day you will ask in my name. I am *not* saying that I will ask the Father on your behalf. No, the Father himself loves you because you have loved me and have believed that I came from God." Then Jesus's disciples said, "Now you are speaking clearly and without figures of speech. Now we can see that you know all things and that you do not even need to have anyone ask you questions. This makes us believe that you came from God." (John 16:25–30)

In this emergency, God gave Israel the Ten Commandments and punishments for breaking them. If you broke one of the commandments, you were in serious *legal* trouble.

And he took the book of the covenant, and read in the audience of the people: and they said, "All that the Lord hath said will we do." And Moses took the blood, and sprinkled it on the people, and said, behold the blood of the covenant. (Exod. 24:7–8, KJV)

The legal aspects of the law were initiated with the people's proclamation: "All that the Lord hath said will we do." There had never been concrete legal consequences attached to the keeping of specific rules until the commandments were given at Mount Sinai. Adam and Eve, Cain and Able, Noah and others offered simple sacrifices in earlier times expressing their sorrow for sin and acknowledging their faith in a redeemer to come. For them, it wasn't to fulfill a "legal" requirement. But now, God had to be blunt. He made the law, clear as crystal, and punishments for breaking them, hard as rock.

CHAPTER 13

The Ten Commandments Accomplish

The law of love stands on two legs—love the Lord your God with all your heart and with all your soul and with all your strength, and love your neighbor as yourself (Deut. 6:5; Lev. 19:18), and it is broken down further into the Ten Commandments. The Ten Commandments are synonymous with the law of love if you consider the principles behind each one; however, most people only read them superficially, at least until Jesus came and explained it to them. It wasn't a proud day for God when He shook and thundered on Mount Sinai and had to tell His children to stop the killing, but He had to do something. The laws and punishments were given to accomplish the following:

1. Give the people a standard to keep, a bar to reach, a picture of good to think about, and something easy to remember.
2. Give the people a barrier against self-destruction. Their current habits were destructive. Doing what is good and right brings positive consequence (when you are truthful with your spouse, you will have a happy home), and avoids negative consequences (when you lie to your spouse, you will not have a happy home).
3. Give the people legal requirements.

If a law was broken, a punishment was imposed. The sinner was to take a lamb to the priest. The priest would hold the animal while the person placed his or her hands on the animal's head and confessed his or her sin, symbolically transferring the sin to the animal. The priest would then slit the animal's throat with a knife and collect some of its blood. The blood would be taken to the altar and eventually into the two-roomed tabernacle, where it would be purged on the Day of Atonement. This legal system includes sanctuary rituals and living parables meant to lift the people's eyes toward a loving, sin-pardoning God. Every time they broke a commandment, they were to kill a lamb, ram, oxen, or dove, which was symbolic of Christ.

CHAPTER 14

———○○◦🙩◦○○———

The Ten Commandments—
Misnomer

T his ceremony does not get a lot of explanation in the Bible and
is the source of a great amount of confusion. What is God
trying to get across to the Israelites? Again, what is the pairing
of sin and death all about? Many believe God is teaching that if you
sin, then someone needs to be punished, and the punishment is death,
and Jesus took your punishment. End of story. But it can be looked at
in a different way. God is reminding His creatures that sin causes death,
and a Messiah would someday demonstrate this truth. Unfortunately,
however, most of the people came to believe that God requires death as
punishment—an *imposed* retribution—but that is a heathen concept;
it came from the ancient mystery religions, and it led to babies being
sacrificed to Moloch the sun god. In short, they misunderstood the
ceremony and the penalty for not keeping the law.

The two concepts—sin causes death, and God requires death—are
as different as night and day in the mind, but outwardly they look
exactly the same. Outside observers wouldn't see the difference if they
were watching the Israelites' sacrificial service. A misunderstanding
of the sacrificial system and a preexisting fear of God leads people to
a wrong interpretation of the meaning of the sacrificial animal. God

was trying to illustrate that lawlessness causes death, not God, and a Messiah was going to come and make it clear someday. There is a very subtle but important difference in the two meanings associated with the sacrificial animal. It is easy to see how the Israelites could get confused, and even easier to see that Satan would love for us to look upon God as a tyrant who requires death as a penalty for each and every sin. Someday, it was prophesied, a Messiah would come to explain it all.

CHAPTER 15

—⚬o⟩◉⟨o⚬—

God Added Rules

In all, God gave seven sets of laws: the Ten Commandments, statutes, health laws, dietary laws, governmental laws, sanctuary laws, and festivals. We have already touched on the moral law and noted that love is eternal, but the Israelites needed help putting them into practice, so God added statutes. These laws were more specific and gave examples of how to implement the Ten Commandments, such as:

> Do not defraud or rob your neighbor. Do not hold back the wages of a hired worker overnight. Do not curse the deaf or put a stumbling block in front of the blind, but fear your God. I am the LORD. (Lev. 19:13–14)

He gave sanitary laws to control diseases such as leprosy (Lev. 14) and dietary laws to help them think, reason, and live long, healthy lives (Lev. 11). He gave laws for governing how to march, how to set up camp, how to handle legal matters, etc. (Deut. 15), and God added rules for the sanctuary service (Lev. 16) and yearly festivals (Lev. 24). The sanctuary service was complex and symbolic of events taking place in heaven.

This set of laws formed the fabric of the nation. It made Israel what they were; it distinguished them from all the other nations. Had the

Israelites bought into God's plan, they would have been the greatest nation on Earth. Morally, mentally, physically, and nationally they would have been without a rival and would have drawn the inquiry of everyone. Why is your country so much better than ours? What do you have that we don't? They could have told them about their wonderful God and vindicated Jehovah and His ways before the universe.

But they didn't follow God's plan, and they didn't vindicate God's principles. In approximately fifteen hundred years their nation will be known only by reading history books, and people will wonder why God gave all those rules and will argue about it.

***

The Israelites corrupt themselves within forty days of God giving Moses the stone tablets. Forgetting that God just shook and thundered, and evidently not nearly enough, they cast off their covenant and worshiped a golden calf. Their celebration was much more than reverently bowing down to a gilded quadruped; they got smashed, and they re-created the erotic worship services they had learned in Egypt—it was more like watching *Animal House.*

> When Moses approached the camp and saw the calf and the dancing, his anger burned and he threw the tablets out of his hands, breaking them to pieces at the foot of the mountain. And he took the calf the people had made and burned it in the fire; then he ground it to powder, scattered it on the water and made the Israelites drink it. (Exod. 32:19–20)
>
> Moses saw that the people were running wild and that Aaron had let them get out of control and so become a laughingstock to their enemies. So he stood at the entrance to the camp and said, "Whoever is for the Lord, come to me." And all the Levites rallied to him.

Then he said to them, "This is what the Lord, the God of Israel, says: 'Each man strap a sword to his side. Go back and forth through the camp from one end to the other, each killing his brother and friend and neighbor.'" The Levites did as Moses commanded, and that day about three thousand of the people died. (Exod. 32:25–28)

God could get the people out of Egypt easy enough; but how can He get Egypt out of the people? This is the fourth time we read about death and the third time we see God use a show of force, and it did not work long-term.

Chapter 16

Lessons of Trust

Wilderness Wondering

The bulk of the Old Testament chronicles God's attempts to inspire faith in Himself, get Israel to behave, and motivate Israel to tell the world about Himself. But the Israelites refused the program and oscillated between being hard-hearted and Laodicean. Consider this story of Israel in the Wilderness.

Shortly after their Ten Commandments primer, God tried to take them straight to the Promised Land. While on the way He took care of them in the desert. He fed them manna and quail. He led them by day with clouds and by night with fire. He protected them from cobras and bandits and disease. But when it was time to go into Canaan, they rebelled. They got to the border and froze, fearing the unknown. Again, the Israelites didn't trust Him enough to do what He asked. Not that they even needed to spy out the land. God told them to go in and take it, and that should have been enough, but when they did go and take a peek, only Joshua and Caleb of the twelve spies brought back a positive, faithful report. The Israelites refused to go forth.

Like when God disciplined Adam and Eve by taking them out of the garden of Eden to learn lessons of trust, so God disciplined the mixed multitude with forty years in the wilderness, a year for each day the spies were in Canaan. For four more decades, God took care of them. God wanted to lead His people across the Jordan River, fast, like ducks to water, but it was more like herding cats. Unfortunately, at the end of their training they didn't trust Him any more than their fathers did.

If you were God, what would you do? You are trying to develop trust in those you are leading, and it is not working. You want them to go into Canaan, enjoy the richness of the land, the good life, but you know that as soon as they do, they will forget their need of you, and you'll be forgotten to their complete demise. Do you make them wander for another generation? Will they learn their lessons if you do, or will you let them go into Canaan and risk it, because you are losing face with the nations around Israel? God said He would take them into the Promised Land, and everyone was watching. Remember, the other nations are God's children, too. God told Israel, you're no better than your fathers, but because I need to say something about Myself, I'll take you in (Ezek. 20:9–14). Even though you are not worthy, and have not learned what you needed to learn, I will keep my promise—I will take you home.

CHAPTER 17

Moses

Another crisis occurs just before the Israelites enter Canaan. The water from the rock that Moses had struck at the beginning of their sojourn dried up, and you can't live very long in the desert without water. The Israelites didn't need it anymore because there was plenty of water in Canaan, but they complained like spoiled children anyway. God then instructed Moses to speak to the rock so it might bring forth water, but instead of just speaking to the rock, Moses impatiently struck it and said, "Hear now, ye rebels; must we fetch you water out of this rock?" (Num. 20:10, KJV) God was gracious and poured out water anyway, but Moses ruined a great object lesson: Christ, the Rock, was only to be struck once by sin's staff, and as "punishment," Moses and Aaron were forbidden to enter Canaan and were to die on Mount Nebo (Deut. 34:1–5).

Why the harsh punishment? Is this just another example of how God punishes sinners? So Moses hit the rock with his staff; the Israelites committed many worse offenses, and God forgave them. Was God angry because Moses had disobeyed? Was God angry because he ruined an object lesson? Or was He making an example of Moses, because he had misrepresented Him, just like Satan did in the beginning? Though disobeying is wrong, and ruining an object lesson is unfortunate, the tragedy of Moses's sin was that he misrepresented God to the people.

God wanted to be seen as kind, generous, and holy to the people, but Moses made God look angry and impatient. Moses was God's friend, and the people knew it. In the people's eyes, if Moses said it, God meant it, and that is all there was to it. I am not trying to minimize Moses's sin, but his misrepresentation of God was infinitely worse than merely disobeying. Which is worse, when you disobey your employer and do a bad job at work, or when you fail someone who loves, trusts, and depends on you? Neither is good, but relational sin is much worse than servant-like disobedience. God could have expressed His disappointment with Moses's "disobedience," but God said it this way:

> Because you did not *trust* in me enough to honor me as holy in the sight of the Israelites, you will not bring this community into the land I give them. (Num. 20:12)

God said Moses breached trust, not obedience. We use terms such as obey and disobey with those we control, such as children, slaves, and dogs. We use terms such as trust, faith, and love with those we respect. For God's friends, Moses, Abraham, Job, and a few select others, God describes sin as a lack of trust. It is not that obeying God is wrong or bad, but God has higher expectations than that. What He would really like is to have thinking, questioning, trusting, and loving friends—people who can honestly and sincerely, love, trust, support, and defend Him.

CHAPTER 18

Joshua

After Aaron's and Moses's death, God opens up the Jordan River, and Joshua escorts the people across on dry ground, to a land swarming with giants and warlike cities. God wanted to chase out the inhabitants with hornets, that way He could select who could stay and who should go, surgically, but Israel wouldn't have it. They wanted an army. They didn't feel safe with an invisible God watching over them and fighting their battles. So God condescended and helped them get organized; He even helped them wipe out the wicked Amorites, Jebusites, and Canaanites out of the land.

Joshua proved to be a courageous leader, but as soon as he was gone, the Israelites slid back down into the muck. They failed to finish the job of casting out the seducing nations around them. Instead of driving them out, they invited them in; they intermarried with them, adopting their customs and their religions and their gods.

Though it seems as if God and the Israelites were going nowhere fast, this is actually a crucial part of the demonstration of what God is like. When circumstances get hard for Israel, when they are going backward and not forward, does God wash His hands of them, bail out of the relationship, and abandon them in their hour of need? No. In fact, even when the Israelites were doing their worst, God stood by them. He may not have won every battle for them or paved each road with glitter, but he stuck with them, helped them, and reminded them of his constant love and concern. Look what God endured during the days of the Judges.

CHAPTER 19

Judges

Most people would agree that some of Israel's darkest days were in the period of the judges. The book is replete with stories of murder, intrigue, uprisings, rebellions, immoral sex, dishonesty—anarchy. If you can name it or think it, it happened in the days of the judges. Judges highlights the acts of Sampson killing thousands with the jawbone of an ass and how he succumbs to Delilah's temptations. It tells how he dies—killing thousands more by pulling down the coliseum columns after having his eyes gouged out. It chronicles the murder of a horribly obese king, a woman who pounds a tent peg through a general's head, and Gideon, who mops up the entire Midianite army with three hundred men. After every judge delivers Israel from its enemies, pathetically, Israel just sinks deeper in sin and rebellion, only to hit bottom, pray for forgiveness, and have God come to the rescue. Perhaps the saddest story is the Levite and his concubine, found in chapter 19.

Levite and His Concubine

A Levite was traveling with his concubine. It was late in the day, and, being afraid of staying the night in a scary heathen town, he decided to travel farther to a city he thought safe, Gibeah, in Benjamin, a city with fellow "godly" Israelite believers. After being taken in by a friendly Benjamite, the townsmen surround the dwelling, and demand that the traveler be brought out so they could have sex with him (reminiscent of Lot in Sodom). The host refuses to let the man out but offers up his virgin daughter and the traveler's concubine. Somehow, only the concubine is sent out, and the lecherous horde raped and abused the woman all night. At first light, the Levite discovered his concubine dead at the door. After taking her home on his donkey, enraged, the Levite chopped her up into twelve chunks, and sent the woman's body parts to the other tribes of Israel to point out their wickedness. This starts a civil war that almost annihilates the tribe of Benjamin.

Why didn't God step in then? What is God doing, or not doing? It is amazing to see what God tolerates from His people at times. Had God not already demonstrated that power and force don't work with the flood, this could have been a good time to bring on the fire and brimstone, but that lesson has already been taught. God has a plan, and He will take care of sin and wickedness when it is time, but chose not to step in at this low point in Israel's history. Little did anyone know there would be a lower point to come.

CHAPTER 20

A Kingdom Divided

Samuel was the last of Israel's good judges and passed the torch to his dishonest sons Joel and Abijah. They used their priestly position like corrupt politicians, taking more than their share of the people's church offerings. Finally, Israel had all they could take of their greed and demanded a king. God warned them it wouldn't be as sweet as they thought, like someone's son joining the Marines because he saw a "Be all you can be" commercial, not knowing he would have to dodge bullets. He warned them that the king they wanted would tax them to death, take their land, take their crops, take their daughters as slaves, and take their sons for war. But they didn't care. They wanted a change. God told Samuel, give the people what they want. They didn't reject you; they rejected Me.

Even though they rejected Jehovah as their leader, God was gracious and pointed out the best king possible, a tall, handsome, wise king, Saul, son of Kish, and God gave him His Spirit. Saul started off well, but unfortunately for Saul and Israel, he became proud, self-confident, rebellious, and faithless to the point that he consulted the dead on behalf of the living, a witch, the infamous witch of Endor (1 Sam. 28:7). Satan used the witch to discourage Saul before going into battle with the Philistines, and, after being shot by an arrow in battle, Saul committed suicide, falling on his sword, and left the kingdom in David's hands (1 Sam. 31:4, 1 Chron. 10:14).

Under most of David's reign and the first part of Solomon's, though it wasn't a walk in the park, Israel prospered, and God was respected, praised, and honored. The ideals God had been attempting to instill in Israel were beginning to be realized. Solomon had visitors come from the far ends of the earth to hear of his wisdom (1 Kings 10). But sadly, mainly because of Solomon's personal demise, Israel crumbled.

Saul, David, and Solomon: in each era we can see how God helped, Satan hindered, and the leaders floundered. Though Solomon started off the wisest man on earth, his love for his seven hundred heathen wives proved his ruin. He erected temples, groomed gardens, and even sacrificed his sons in worship services to Molech (1 Kings 11). These attractive religions seduced Solomon and the nation into idolatry—again. After Solomon's multiple personal and political disasters, the dynasty was looked upon with contempt. Israel was a train wreck looking for a place to happen. When the leaders led well, the people followed well. When their leaders failed, the people were not far behind. There are many lessons to be learned, but one is unmistakable. People rarely rise higher than their leaders. What kind of leader was Lucifer?

CHAPTER 21

‒‒∘∘∘‒◄●►‒∘∘∘‒

The Kingdom Splits

Approximately 345 years and twelve generations span the time from when Israel split in two and when Judah was finally destroyed by Babylon (586 BC). During this period, Israel did horrendous things, things even the pagan nations thought perverse, yet Israel still had the gall to say, "How have we shown contempt for Your name?" as they wandered back from worshiping at pagan temples. Consider this text from Amos:

> "Hear this word, you cows of Bashan on Mount Samaria, you women who oppress the poor and crush the needy and say to your husbands, "Bring us some drinks!" The Sovereign Lord has sworn by his holiness: "The time will surely come when you will be taken away with hooks, the last of you with fishhooks. You will each go straight out through breaches in the wall, and you will be cast out toward Harmon," declares the Lord. "Go to Bethel and sin; go to Gilgal and sin yet more. Bring your sacrifices every morning, your tithes every three years. Burn leavened bread as a thank offering and brag about your freewill offerings—boast about them, you Israelites, for this is what you love to do," declares the

Sovereign Lord. "I gave you empty stomachs in every city and lack of bread in every town, *yet you have not returned to me,*" declares the Lord. (Amos 4:1–6)

The Israelites had a foot on both sides of the fence. They were doing what they thought God wanted them to do, but without heart. Like galley slaves, they were only doing what they thought they had to do. They only did what little they did out of a sense of obligation. They wouldn't have brought Him offerings except they thought God demanded it, and the same is true with giving a tithe, giving burnt offerings, going to church, singing hymns, and praying. They were also singing and praying and offering sacrifices to the gods of the Ammonites, Hittites, and Canaanites. Amos continues:

This is what the Lord says to Israel: "*Seek me and live;* do not seek Bethel, do not go to Gilgal, do not journey to Beersheba. ... Seek good, not evil, that you may live. Then the Lord God Almighty will be with you, just as you say he is. Hate evil, love good; maintain justice in the courts. Perhaps the Lord God Almighty will have mercy on the remnant of Joseph. ... "*I hate, I despise your religious festivals*; your assemblies are a stench to me. Even though you bring me burnt offerings and grain offerings, I will not accept them. Though you bring choice fellowship offerings, I will have no regard for them. Away with the *noise of your songs!* I will not listen to the music of your harps. *But let justice roll on like a river, righteousness like a never-failing stream!*" (Amos 5)

It was God that "commanded" that they come and worship. It was God that told them to tithe and go to church and give sacrifices, but they missed the point. These things were supposed to lead them to an intimate relationship with God—"seek Me and live"—but the Israelites misunderstood God and thought He was only interested in their legal performance. They thought God only required outward obedience and didn't care about the heart and motives. And did you notice, it was the priests leading the way down.

Some say the Old Testament isn't as clear as the New Testament when it comes to knowing what God is like and what God wants from his children, but Micah 6:1–8 makes it very clear.

> "My people, *what have I done to you? How have I burdened you?* Answer me. I brought you up out of Egypt and redeemed you from the land of slavery. I sent Moses to lead you, also Aaron and Miriam."

Micah speaking for the people:

> With what shall I come before the Lord and bow down before the exalted God? Shall I come before him with burnt offerings, with calves a year old? Will the Lord be pleased with thousands of rams, with ten thousand rivers of olive oil? Shall I offer my firstborn for my transgression, the fruit of my body for the sin of my soul? He has shown you, O mortal, what is good. And what does the Lord require of you? *To act justly and to love mercy and to walk humbly with your God.* (Mic. 6:1–8)

Micah, speaking for the people, said, "With what shall I come before the Lord?" That is to say, I know we have done wickedly and have forgotten You, but we want to come back; we want to come home. But how? What should we bring? What should we do? If You are happy with one sacrifice (which God commanded them to do), will ten make you happier, what about ten thousand? Do you understand the hyperbole? What is God's reply? I don't want sacrifices; I want your hearts. I don't want you to sacrifice lambs and bulls and goats. Do the right things, love mercy, and be willing to listen humbly to your God.

CHAPTER 22

Success?

The closing years of the Ten Northern Tribes were characterized by extreme violence. For two hundred years they stubbornly went their own way, casting off their allegiance to Jehovah, worshiping idols and objects of nature. King after king ascended the throne via a bloody path, and at the end, without receiving God's help, Israel was ravaged then scattered by Assyria. God worked hard to win over Israel before their doom. He sent Elisha, Elijah, Amos, and Hosea to wake them out of their rebellious stupor, but God finally had to proclaim,

> "My people are hell-bent on leaving me" (Hosea 11:7, MSG), and "Ephraim is joined to idols; leave him alone!" (Hosea 4:17)

Through Amos, He pleaded,

> "Seek me and live (Amos 5:4) Seek good, and not evil, that you may live; and so the Lord, the God of hosts, will be with you, as you have said. Hate evil, and love good, and establish justice in the gate; it may be that the

> Lord, the God of hosts, will be gracious to the remnant
> of Joseph. (Amos 5:14–15)

But they did not listen.

The destruction of Israel came gradually. At first, when Pul, the king of Assyria, came against Israel they allowed Israel to operate as a vassal. Assyria invaded Israel two more times, with the final blow coming from Shalmaneser, who laid siege around the capital, Samaria. They killed thousands with hunger, disease, and the sword, and scattered the survivors over hundreds of miles in Assyria.

One hundred years after the ten northern Tribes of Israel were mauled by Assyria, the two southern Tribes of Judah repeated Israel's performance with Babylon. Micah exclaimed, "The good man is perished out of the earth; and there is none upright among men. The best of them is as a brier: the most upright is sharper than a thorn hedge" (Mic. 7:2–4).

Judah was disciplined slowly by the armies of Nebuchadnezzar. First, Judah was attacked, and only a few captives were taken to the land of Shinar, but later thousands, and then tens of thousands, are exiled. More and more severe were the punishments laid upon Judah.

Eventually, Judah became a wasteland. The city was sieged. Jerusalem was burned, and the magnificent temple that Solomon had built was destroyed. Those that didn't starve to death inside the gates and were able to flee the city were saved only to be captured or killed by a Babylonian sword. Through it all the prophet Jeremiah had counseled King Zedekiah to give in to the Babylonians' demands, promising that the people would be spared if he complied. But the proud, vacillating king was too weak in character. Pandering to his arrogant advisors, he refused to surrender to Babylon.

Jeremiah was shown kindness by his captors, knowing how he had counseled Zedekiah to give up, and was allowed to stay in Judah with a few of his countrymen. But instead of staying around to keep the weeds down and the jackals at bay, the remnant demand that they wait it out in Egypt. Jeremiah protested, wanting them to stay in Canaan, but they went anyway. Depressed, Jeremiah writes the book of Lamentations.

How deserted lies the city, once so full of people!
How like a widow is she, who once was great among the
nations!

She who was queen among the provinces has now
become a slave.

Bitterly she weeps at night, tears are on her cheeks.
Among all her lovers there is no one to comfort her.
All her friends have betrayed her; they have become her
enemies. (Lam. 1:1–2)

During the next seventy years Babylon is conquered by the Meads, who were conquered by the Persians only to share power. Daniel is promoted to the third-highest rank in the kingdom; much like Joseph did in Egypt, and by God's direct intervention escapes from a lion's den. And Shadrach, Meshach, and Abednego declare to a vast crowd of dignitaries that they would rather die in a furnace and worship Jehovah than live and bow down to King Nebuchadnezzar. What God couldn't get Israel to do while free, they do in captivity—they tell their captors about their wonderful God and the promised Messiah, and they stop worshiping idols. It may have taken five hundred years or so, and a lot of tough-love discipline, but God finally ousted "Egypt" from Israel.

CHAPTER 23

‑‑oo‑◖◗‑oo‑‑

Going Home

I t wasn't as spectacular as when God sent the ten plagues and parted the Red Sea, but Israel's exit out of Babylon was not without drama. It took place in three waves, took 160 years, and God thwarted an attempted mass execution by Satan.

At the end of the seventy years of discipline, God motivated King Cyrus to release all those that wanted to go back home to Israel with Governor Zerubbabel, to rebuild the temple. But of the potential million exiles, only fifty thousand wanted to go home. Fifty thousand won't fill a football stadium, much less the country. You would think they would be counting the seconds to the end of Jeremiah's prophesy, and every man, woman, and child would be making tracks out of Babylon. But they didn't. This event splits Israel in two: some go to Jerusalem, but most stay in Persia.

Satan tried to discourage those who went back to Jerusalem with diplomatic tactics. He caused delay after delay. What could have taken just five years to complete took eighty. But worse yet, he tries to kill those who stay behind in Babylon with a death decree. Who knows, maybe the Messiah will be born from those who never left?

Satan has inspired at least three mass murders: Pharaoh's decree at the time of Moses, the death decree that Esther spoiled in Babylon, and the decree to kill all the babies in Jerusalem at the time of Jesus's birth.

And who knows how many others he has inspired around the world? He may have inspired Hitler, Stalin, Pol Pot, and others. The Bible also says that he will try again. Just before Christ comes again, he'll try to silence those who dare to defy him (Rev. 13).

In this death decree, on the thirteenth day of Adar (twelfth month) all of the Israelites living in Babylon were to be killed. But God worked through Esther, a faithful young Jewish woman, to bring the decree upon their enemies' heads. What would have been almost total annihilation for the Jews ended up killing over seventy-five thousand of their enemies.

All this happened before the next wave of refugees go back to Jerusalem with Ezra. This time, two thousand exiles make the nine-hundred-mile journey home. And finally, thirteen years later, Nehemiah leads another group of Jews back to Jerusalem.

In this 160-year period they rebuild the temple, though it was just a shadow of Solomon's edifice. Then they rebuild the city, the city wall, the city gates, and, more significantly, they find the lost Old Testament scrolls.

The scrolls had actually been hidden so they wouldn't be captured or burned when Nebuchadnezzar laid siege against Jerusalem. That was almost 230 years ago. The scrolls were everything!

> All the people came together as one in the square before the Water Gate. They told Ezra the teacher of the Law to bring out the Book of the Law of Moses, which the Lord had commanded for Israel. … He read it aloud from daybreak till noon as he faced the square before the Water Gate in the presence of the men, women, and others who could understand. And all the people listened attentively to the Book of the Law. … Then Nehemiah the governor, Ezra the priest and teacher of the Law, and the Levites who were instructing the people said to them all, "This day is holy to the Lord your God. Do not mourn or weep." *For all the people had been weeping as they listened to the words of the Law.* (Neh. 8:1–9)

This revival is one of the last stories in the Old Testament; only the stories in Malachi come later. And what a revival! It transformed the Israelites. Ezra read to them the words that Moses spoke to Israel before going into Canaan—the blessings and cursings. It was a warning that if they forgot God and went their own way, there would be dire consequences. Read some of what they heard, and you'll understand why they were crying:

> But it shall come to pass, if you do not obey the voice of the Lord your God, to observe carefully all His commandments and His statutes which I command you today; that all these curses will come upon you and overtake you: Cursed *shall you be* in the city, and cursed *shall you be* in the country. Cursed *shall be* your basket and your kneading bowl. Cursed *shall be* the fruit of your body and the produce of your land. ...

> The Lord will cause you to be defeated before your enemies; you shall go out one way against them and flee seven ways before them; and you shall become troublesome to all the kingdoms of the earth. ... A nation whom you have not known shall eat the fruit of your land and the produce of your labor, and you shall be only oppressed and crushed continually. The Lord will bring you and the king whom you set over you to a nation which neither you nor your fathers have known, and there you shall serve other gods—wood and stone. And you shall become an astonishment, a proverb, and a byword among all nations where the Lord will drive you. ...

> Therefore you shall serve your enemies, whom the Lord will send against you, in hunger, in thirst, in nakedness, and in need of everything; and He will put a yoke of iron on your neck until He has destroyed you. The Lord will bring a nation against you from afar, from the end of the

earth, as swift as the eagle flies, a nation whose language you will not understand, a nation of fierce countenance, which does not respect the elderly nor show favor to the young. ...

They shall besiege you at all your gates until your high and fortified walls, in which you trust, come down throughout all your land; and they shall besiege you at all your gates throughout all your land which the Lord your God has given you. ...

Then the Lord will scatter you among all peoples, from one end of the earth to the other, and there you shall serve other gods, which neither you nor your fathers have known—wood and stone. (Deut. 28:15–64)

Those standing in the rain listening to Ezra knew they had experienced the bitter fulfillment of Moses's words. They had become a proverb and a byword, a stench among the nations.

What do you think the Israelites learned from their Babylonian gulag experience? What did they learn from Ezra's reading of the Torah? At a minimum, I don't think they wanted an instant replay of those seventy years. Now they took God seriously. Now they took sin seriously. And now they took His Law and ceremonies seriously. God finally had a people who attempted to follow His ways. For the first time—ever—en masse, the people worshiped Jehovah and not some heathen deity. God had at last obtained a group of truly obedient servants.

At this point in time we should ask if the questions about God have been sufficiently answered. Is God arbitrary in His decrees? Is He exacting in His requirements? Is He unforgiving when approached? Is He severe with His discipline? And can we tell if He has lied about sin causing death? It doesn't matter how you answered, the clearest answers are still to come.

CHAPTER 24

Intertestament Period

Another four hundred years produced the Jews who greeted Jesus when He was born in Bethlehem. What happened in that intertestament period that could produce people so zealous for keeping God's laws, but who are so clueless as to who God is or what He is like that they could kill Him?

Though not written in the Bible, some major events are generally agreed upon. After leaving their Babylonian captivity, the Hebrews organized the Old Testament doctrines by topic, in an oral code known as the *Mishnah*. They decided they were never going to be abandoned by God again for not keeping the law, so they put it to memory. The Mishnah was taught orally from rabbi to student and wasn't written down (redacted) until the first century AD. Today we can read these teachings in the Talmud; it was written down sometime in the fourth century AD, and takes the Mishnah, and then expounds upon it (*Gemara*). Though well-meaning, the oral tradition added additional prohibitions so a person couldn't come close to breaking God's laws. The Babylonian Talmud, as translated by Michael L. Rodkinson (1918), is 3,225 pages. Here is an excerpt concerning what may and may not be worn by animals on the Sabbath:

Mishnah:
What gear may we let animals go about in and what
not? The male camel in a bridle; the female camel with
a nose-ring; Lybian asses in a halter, and a horse in
a collar. All (animals) that are used to collars may go
out in and may be led by the collar. Such gear (when
it becomes defiled) can be sprinkled and submerged
without being removed from its (proper) place (on the
animal).

Gemara:
Rabbi Jehudah in the name of Samuel said: "Rabbi
was asked how it is when the reverse is the case? *i.e.*,
when the female camel is bridled and the male camel is
invested with a nose-ring? May they be allowed to go
about? There is no question as to a bridle on a female
camel, for it is considered a burden; as to a nose-ring
on a male camel, shall we assume that it is merely an
additional safeguard, and thus becomes permissible, or
is it an unnecessary safeguard and hence not allowed?"

R. Ishmael B. Jossi answered: "Thus my father said:
Four animals may go about with a bridle on—the horse,
the mule, the camel, and the ass." A. Boraitha states:
Lydda asses and camels may go about with a bridle on.
The following Tanaim, however, differ as to this point
(whether a superfluous safeguard is a burden or not): one
maintains that no animal may go about burdened with
a chain; but Hananya says a chain or anything else that
is intended as a safeguard is permitted.

The Talmud has rules for everything: what knots to use on the
Sabbath, how far to walk on the Sabbath, even how much rope you
can carry on the Sabbath. You couldn't even water plants. When Jesus
spit on the ground to make clay, the day He anointed the blind man's
eyes, well, He might as well have drained the whole reservoir. In their

eyes, He was irrigating; He was breaking the Sabbath. The Mishnah must have, at least in part, led to Israel's preoccupation with the rules.

There were also at least three complete regime changes: the Persians were conquered by Alexander the Great (Greece) circa 330 BC. Greece split into four realms, each territory eventually succumbing to Rome, with Jerusalem falling in 63 BC. Each kingdom came with its own language, customs, and religions. The Jewish nation fought desperately to maintain its individuality while it was dominated by these dynasties. Only once was Israel independent, and that was a short, turbulent period led by the Maccabees.

During a Greek upheaval around 301 BC, many of the Jews left Palestine to settle in Alexandria, Egypt. There, the Jewish population thrived and became so Hellenized that they needed the Hebrew scriptures translated into Greek. They did it and called it the *Septuagint*—the seventy. Legend has it that six translators from each of the twelve tribes of Israel (seventy-two) translated the Torah in seventy-two days and each version came out identical (Marsh 2010). As time went on, those living in Alexandria incorporated additional books into their canon. The Jews living in Palestine never adopted these books, and these were not part of the scriptures that Jesus read, but many Jews were influenced by these writings. These extra books helped alter, subtly, Israel's self-awareness, their view of what Israel was in God's eyes, or at least reflected their changing views of themselves as God's favored nation. They made themselves out to be much more important than the nations around them and, in doing so, distorted their view of God, the coming Messiah, and Israel as a nation. These additional books emphasized zeal for Israel and miracles, especially miracles with pious Jews saving Israel in dramatic ways.

Consider the apocryphal story of Judith. An amazingly beautiful young widow named Judith (meaning "Jewess") saves her city from a military siege. She sneaks out of the city, an Israelite stronghold fearing its imminent destruction, and creeps into the enemy camp as though she is defecting. Over several days she allures, then seduces the Assyrian captain with her charm, gets him drunk, and then while he sleeps, slices off his head. Returning to her walled city, she shows his head to her people, goading the men to go out and smash the enemy, which they do with passion. Throughout this story Judith is cast as a very pious woman who is zealous for her race and scrupulously observes all the Laws of Moses.

During this time period many competing religious sects emerge. There were the Sadducees, generally of the ruling upper class, who were considered too liberal by the rest. They rejected the Mishnah and only accepted the books of Moses, as inspired, and they didn't believe in a resurrection or angels. There were the Pharisees, strict conservatives who seemed to give Jesus the most trouble when He came; they were scrupulous law keepers and believed wholeheartedly in the oral traditions. There were the Essenes, who were the most conservative; they were communal, austere, and dedicated themselves to poverty, daily ritual cleansings, and fasting. They abstained from alcohol and other "worldly" attractions, and many were celibate. Finally, there were the Zealots, extremists who wanted to take matters into their own hands and overthrow the Romans by force. These splintered groups made up the fabric of Jewish society and culture.

The combining effects of the Babylonian captivity, Ezra's revival, a codification and amplification of the law in the Mishnah, the acceptance of apocryphal books emphasizing patriotic, nationalistic Israel, the religious splintering of society, and a four-hundred-year barrage of enemies produced the first-century Jews that greeted Jesus. These acquired rules, stereotypes, and nationalistic influences helped shape the nation's concept of what the Messiah would be: a scrupulous law keeper; a zealot; a warrior ready to defend the nation at any cost; powerful, able to topple Israel's oppressive enemies, and who with a look could compel the nations to kneel at Israel's feet. Israel was really looking for Barabbas.

CHAPTER 25

The First-Century Jews

For the first time, God had a people He could call His own, a people who looked like they were devoted to His cause, and who at least outwardly kept the rules. They were Sabbath-keeping, tithe-paying, health-reforming, and scripture-believing people looking for the Messiah's coming—but they only had the law of love on the outside, and they didn't know God. They had never become His understanding friends. They hadn't asked the question: Why?

- Why, God, did You give all the rules about sacrifices when what you really want is faith?
- Why did You have us kill those animals in sacrifices when you hate killing?
- Why didn't You want us to associate with other nations when they are your children too?
- Why did You give us a king when You wanted to be our king?
- Why did You help our army when you wanted to fight our battles with hornets?
- Why did You give us rules for eating animals when you preferred we eat fruits, nuts, grains, and manna?
- Why did You allow divorce when you hate divorce?

- Why did You give us an intercessor when both Moses and Jesus said you love us?

If they had asked, there could have been an alternate ending to the story. They did not have to be the ones clamoring for Christ's death, but they were only servants doing what they thought was demanded of them by an arbitrary, exacting, unforgiving, and severe God. They wouldn't have described God in those terms; they wouldn't have dared, but in their words and actions that is how they portrayed Him. Their relationship to God was formal, legal, and servant-like. They never asked God questions; they just did what they thought the Master demanded. This is a crucial insight! God was going to speak volumes to the onlooking universe regarding the hazards of a formal, legal, servant relationship.

Let me pause to reinforce the gravity of the situation. What God has allowed to happen over these four thousand years is what God warned the angels about when sin was introduced in heaven. God said the wages of sin is death, but He never really explained it. He chose instead to show it. What will sin do to angels or people? Are the results of sin fast or slow, obvious or insidious? What is so bad about wanting your own way and disregarding our loving God's gentle leadership? What's wrong with obeying God out of fear—you're still obeying, aren't you? In AD 30, God was finally going to answer the questions—Himself.

And to do this, to demonstrate clearly what needed to be exposed, Providence brought two cultures into contact. He pitted the cruelest, the most worldly, and the most brutal kingdom to date, against His professed people who had memorized, "Love the Lord your God with all your heart and with all your soul and with all your strength." and, "love your neighbor as yourself." He contrasted a culture who worshiped a vast number of Roman gods and Caesar, to the monotheistic Jews, who claimed they worshiped only Jehovah. He compared the pride and pomp and power of the city set on Seven Hills, to Jerusalem, the city of peace. He pitted man's laws against the laws of heaven. He stacked up the best the world had to offer against those that said they knew God Almighty. And who looked better in the end? And why? Was it God's fault? What happened?

CHAPTER 26

Jesus Answers Questions

Imagine you are back in college working on a law degree, and it is time for your final exam. You have studied well what your professors have taught, but you know you don't know the Constitution and Bill of Rights like you should, and someone looking like George Washington or Thomas Jefferson knocks on the door of your university, and graciously asks for an opportunity to explain what was meant when it was written back in 1787. He says he can tell you the background to why each amendment was written and why it is stated in those precise terms. Your professor agrees and gives him the lectern.

He stands stately at the head of the lecture hall and begins his dissertation, describing in minute detail how it all fits together, but it doesn't sound anything like what your professors have said. In fact, he's 180 degrees off on most things, reversing the meaning of some words, and giving other words an uncomfortable twist. Partway through he is rudely interrupted, and the interruptions continue time and again. He's heckled at the end and leaves your school disgraced. With his head hanging, he leaves hoping to make it clearer at some other university. He interviews on CNBC, CBS, and FOX News, and is cheered-on by the common people. With his popularity rising, he is asked to explain his theories before a joint session of Congress. Answering every question, quoting every source, answering logic with logic, he paints the clearest picture ever given. But the stuffed shirts don't like what he has to say. They claim he's a charlatan, a phony, and not someone you can trust.

What do you think the onlooking leaders would do? What would you do? We know what the first-century Jewish leaders would do—they'd kill him!

Chapter 27

The Author Comes to Explain

The author of the Old Testament came to explain what the thirty-nine books meant and what God was really like, but was despised and rejected as a fake messiah. They loved His miracles but hated His teachings; they loved the "steaks," but despised His picture of God. Right from the start, Jesus faced an uphill battle. Even His famous Sermon on the Mount speech was rejected as unbiblical.

> Now when Jesus saw the crowds, he went up on a mountainside and sat down. His disciples came to him, and he began to teach them.
>
> Blessed are the poor in spirit, for theirs is the kingdom of heaven.
> Blessed are those who mourn, for they will be comforted.
> Blessed are the meek, for they will inherit the earth.
> Blessed are those who hunger and thirst for righteousness, for they will be filled.
> Blessed are the merciful, for they will be shown mercy.
> Blessed are the pure in heart, for they will see God.
> Blessed are the peacemakers, for they will be called children of God.

Blessed are those who are persecuted because of righteousness, for theirs is the kingdom of heaven. Blessed are you when people insult you, persecute you and falsely say all kinds of evil against you because of me. Rejoice and be glad, because great is your reward in heaven, for in the same way they persecuted the prophets who were before you.

You are the salt of the earth. But if the salt loses its saltiness, how can it be made salty again? It is no longer good for anything, except to be thrown out and trampled underfoot.

You are the light of the world. A town built on a hill cannot be hidden. Neither do people light a lamp and put it under a bowl. Instead they put it on its stand, and it gives light to everyone in the house. In the same way, let your light shine before others, that they may see your good deeds and glorify your Father in heaven. (Matt. 5:1–16)

Just two minutes into His lecture Jesus has to pause. He could see they were squirming like worms on a hook. He knew they were not accepting what He had to say. He had to stop and tell them He had not come to do away with the Old Testament, but to explain it.

Do not think that I have come to abolish the Law or the Prophets; I have not come to abolish them but to fulfill them. For truly I tell you, until heaven and earth disappear, not the smallest letter, not the least stroke of a pen, will by any means disappear from the Law until everything is accomplished. Therefore anyone who sets aside one of the least of these commands and teaches others accordingly will be called least in the kingdom of heaven, but whoever practices and teaches these commands will be called great in the kingdom of heaven. For I tell you that unless your righteousness surpasses that of the Pharisees and the teachers of the law, you will certainly not enter the kingdom of heaven. (Matt. 5:17–20)

Jesus said, "Think not that I have come to abolish the Old Testament. I have not come to abolish it; I have come to fulfill it." And He didn't mean that He had come to merely fulfill prophesy. Jesus came to explain the scriptures.

For example: Blessed are the poor in spirit (happy are the poor). Those listening on had been taught that if a man was poor, he was cursed, not blessed. And why was he cursed? Because he was bad. Remember, in the book of Job, as long as Job was making money and healthy, his friends knew he was a good man, but as soon as he lost everything, the three theologians said he must have done something horrible. Their idea was, if you are good, you are blessed, and if you are bad, God curses you.

This is also why Jesus shocked them when he said, "It is easier for a camel to go through the eye of a needle than for a rich man to be saved;" and, "unless your righteousness surpasses that of the Pharisees and the teachers of the law, you will certainly not enter the kingdom of heaven." No one was richer than the Pharisees and Sadducees, and no one was as pious! If they couldn't get into heaven, who could? They thought Jesus was out of his mind. But their theology was wrong. The book of Job was supposed to correct that view, but it was not being taught in the synagogues. Job was good, and he lost everything, but they missed that lesson.

The very first thing Jesus preached on was considered heresy, but it was true. They thought He was not in harmony with the Old Testament, but He was.

They did not like his teachings, but were they new?

You have heard that it was said to the people long ago, "You shall not murder, and anyone who murders will be subject to judgment." But I tell you that anyone who is angry with a brother or sister will be subject to judgment. (Matt. 5:21–22)

Did Jesus say that for the first time, or did Moses say it in Leviticus 19:17?

You shall not hate your brother in your heart.

And what about adultery?

You have heard that it was said, "You shall not commit adultery." But I tell you that anyone who looks at a woman lustfully has already committed adultery with her in his heart. (Matt. 5:27)

Is this new or was it in the Old Testament already? Doesn't the tenth commandment say thou shall not covet—that there should be no evil desires?

You shall not covet your neighbor's house. You shall not covet your neighbor's wife, or his male or female servant, his ox or donkey, or anything that belongs to your neighbor. (Exod. 20:17; Deut. 5:21)

You don't really have the law in your heart when you merely stop breaking the rules. You need to not even want to do those evil acts. The tenth commandment prohibits even having evil desires. If you want it, you're not keeping the Ten. Jesus did not give new commands. He just explained the ones already written down.

Then He moves to divorce.

It has been said, "Anyone who divorces his wife must give her a certificate of divorce." But I tell you that anyone who divorces his wife, except for sexual immorality, makes her the victim of adultery, and anyone who marries a divorced woman commits adultery. (Matt. 5:32)

That lesson was hard to take. No one liked what He said. His disciples didn't like it, and neither did the Pharisees, who brought it up later. And remember, the Pharisees really wanted to be saved; they wanted to follow all the rules.

> Some Pharisees came to him to test him. They asked, "Is it lawful for a man to divorce his wife for any and every reason? (Matt. 19:3)

And Jesus replied in a very significant way. He did not give them a quick proof text ... not even two proof texts. He said the only way I can answer this question is to go back to the beginning.

> "Haven't you read," he replied, "that at the beginning the Creator made them male and female, and said, 'For this reason a man will leave his father and mother and be united to his wife, and the two will become one flesh?' So they are no longer two, but one flesh. Therefore what God has joined together, let no one separate."(Matt. 19:4–6)

The Pharisees were thinking in their minds, we have several Old Testament scriptures to quote showing God approves of divorce, such as Deuteronomy 24:1–4 and Ezra 10:9–11. How can Jesus say otherwise? The Pharisees asked Jesus:

> Why then ... did Moses command that a man give his wife a certificate of divorce and send her away? (Matt. 19:7)

Jesus replied:

> Moses permitted you to divorce your wives because your hearts were hard. But it was not this way from the beginning. I tell you that anyone who divorces his wife, except for sexual immorality, and marries another woman commits adultery. (Matt 19:8–9)

In this reply Jesus sets the stage for understanding what God wants regarding many of the questions the Pharisees raised: why did Moses or Isaiah or Jeremiah or … say that? It is a compromise—a concession—an emergency measure; He was meeting people where they were. What He wanted was really much better. Why was there so much confusion regarding His teachings? Why did they seem so different from the Old Testament? They didn't understand that the scriptures are not just a rule book. The scriptures are the record of how God has handled the war; it's a demonstration of what God is like, and how God has managed, case by case, His children's rebellion.

Chapter 28

Arbitrary, Exacting,
Unforgiving, and Severe

What else did the Teacher come to tell us? Will we listen and understand any better two thousand years later? Are our hearts any softer than the Pharisees? Are we any less stuck in tradition than they were? I know we are better off historically; at least we agree that Jesus was the true Messiah and God with us. We don't need to debate whether what Jesus said is true. It is true. And we should listen. But some of His greatest teachings are not in His sermons but in His actions. Once, He brought a little girl back to life and reminded her parents to go and get her something to eat. Jesus cared about everything and everyone, even to the smallest details. Great instruction has also come from what Jesus did not do, like when He refused to be crowned a king (John 6).

Jesus had just finished healing the diseased people brought to Him from the regions around the Sea of Galilee, and then He fed about five thousand men, plus women and children, with five barley loaves and two small fish. After seeing the miracle, the people tried to force Jesus to be king, not because of His genuine love and kindness, not because of His sterling character, and not because of His charismatic ability to lead and inspire, but because they saw in Him someone who could feed armies, heal wounded soldiers, and win battles—they wanted a warrior who could break the yoke of Rome—and Jesus wouldn't have any of it. He didn't come to earth to win political or military battles. Jesus came to earth to win hearts over to God.

Did Jesus ever address the questions raised by Satan in the garden of Eden?

Is God Arbitrary?

Being called arbitrary is not a compliment. It suggests you're inconsistent or capricious, that sometimes the answer is yes and sometimes no, and for no good reason. It also implies you don't really care whether the result will do good or evil.

Some people are arbitrary in the way they hide behind their authority. There are no good reasons for what they want. They say, "Do it because I said so," or "do it because I'm your father," or "believe me because I have a PhD." Other people actually want you to bolster their ego or do things so they don't have to, because they are lazy. Does God ever use these shortcuts? Does God ever ask us to believe what He says on the basis of His authority alone?

After His death and resurrection, Jesus wanted to help explain to some of His followers what had just transpired in Jerusalem:

Two men were traveling to a village named Emmaus and talking about what had happened that day in the city. Jesus himself came up and walked along with them, but He didn't reveal who He was. He asked them why they were so sad. Astonished that He didn't know what had occurred that day, they replied, "Jesus of Nazareth was a prophet, powerful in speech and action, and they crucified him; we had hoped that he was the Messiah." And without revealing who He was, He opened the Scriptures to their understanding. Only later, after

He showed them the evidence, and they were convinced of it, did Jesus reveal who He was (Luke 24:13–27).

On the road to Emmaus, Jesus could have told the two disciples walking with Him that He was the risen Savior, showed them the scars in His hands, feet, and side, and overwhelmed them with His authority to prove that the One crucified was the Messiah, but He didn't. Jesus took them through the evidence of the Old Testament before He revealed who He was.

This is also why Jesus said it was better for Him to leave and send the Holy Spirit in His place. If Jesus were to have stayed after His miraculous resurrection, everyone would go to Him for answers, and we would believe what He said just because of who was telling us. We wouldn't have ever grown up and learned to discern truth for ourselves. We would be sitting ducks if someone was to impersonate Christ and tell us lies, and we were accustomed to getting all our answers that way. This way, because we can't see Christ or the Holy Spirit, He can lead us to the truth, but we won't be influenced by His personal testimony. This way we are forced to read the biblical record for ourselves and compare the truth unbiased by either Christ's or Satan's personal influence. We truly get to make up our own minds as to what God is like and whether God can be trusted.

Jesus showed that God does not exercise arbitrary control, use manipulative measures, or lay arbitrary rules upon His children—He doesn't need to. His ways are perfect. He always does the right thing. He respects His children's freedom to choose and their autonomy. God doesn't hide behind an arbitrary cloak.

Is God Exacting?

One of Jesus's teachings—the rich young ruler—has been looked upon as exacting by some.

> One day a rich man came to Jesus and asked: "Teacher, what good thing must I do to get eternal

97

life?" Jesus replied, "If you want to enter life, keep the commandments." "Which ones?" he inquired. Jesus replied, "'You shall not murder, you shall not commit adultery, you shall not steal, you shall not give false testimony, honor your father and mother,' and 'love your neighbor as yourself.'" "All these I have kept," the young man said. "What do I still lack?" Jesus answered, "If you want to be perfect, go, sell your possessions and give to the poor, and you will have treasure in heaven. Then come, follow me." When the young man heard this, he went away sad, because he had great wealth. (Matt. 19:16–22)

Jesus's reply, *"If you want to be perfect, go, sell your possessions and give to the poor,"* may seem extreme and exacting. I remember when I first read this verse. I didn't know what to do, but I could tell it called for a decision. The rich young ruler didn't think he was lacking in righteousness and wanted to justify himself in front of the others. He had been doing all the right things, "from his youth," but not with the best motives—he was self-righteous. Jesus, reading his character, pointed out the blight—he didn't have a true love for God or people, and really didn't believe in Christ; if he had, he would have marched off and done it. Jesus asked him to choose between the nickel-plated riches of this world and the Pearl of Great Price—between serving himself and serving God. The real issue was not about the man's money, but his heart. One more item shouldn't be overlooked. Jesus was asking the young man to change his theology, his picture of God, specifically, his idea that God blessed good people and cursed bad people. Jesus touched on this in his sermon on the Mount of Olives and wanted to repeat the lesson.

The popular thought was, if you were rich, it was because you were doing the right things—you were righteous—and God had blessed you because of it. Thus, you would be saved. Being rich, then, was synonymous with going to heaven. If he listened to Jesus and sold what he had, he would no longer appear rich; he would apparently not be receiving God's blessings, and look lost, not saved. In other words, if he sold all he had and followed Jesus, he would lose the evidence of his salvation, but He didn't trust Jesus enough to take that chance.

It may seem exacting to require someone to give up all his or her possessions, but this request was not given to everyone. Even if it were, we would be trading our broken seashells for pearls. What God has to offer is beyond compare to the shallow-minded treasures we hold on to. God has never asked us to give up something for which He hasn't given back much more or which wasn't in our best interest. I cannot find one instance where Jesus could be considered exacting, demanding, finicky, or picky. Just the opposite; He is flexible, generous, accommodating, and easygoing. Even the new commandment He gave is not exacting: "Love one another. As I have loved you, so you must love one another." (John 13:34)

Is God Unforgiving?

At dawn he [Jesus] appeared again in the temple courts,
where all the people gathered around him, and he sat
down to teach them. The teachers of the law and the
Pharisees brought in a woman caught in adultery. They
made her stand before the group and said to Jesus,
"Teacher, this woman was caught in the act of adultery.
In the Law Moses commanded us to stone such women.

Now what do you say?" They were using this question as a trap, in order to have a basis for accusing him. But Jesus bent down and started to write on the ground with his finger. When they kept on questioning him, he straightened up and said to them, "Let any one of you who is without sin be the first to throw a stone at her." Again he stooped down and wrote on the ground. At this, those who heard began to go away one at a time, the older ones first, until only Jesus was left, with the woman still standing there. Jesus straightened up and asked her, "Woman, where are they? Has no one condemned you?" "No one, sir," she said. *"Then neither do I condemn you,"* Jesus declared. *"Go now and leave your life of sin."* (John 8:2–11)

For most people looking on, this was a cut and dry case. Not that any of those watching were pure, but adultery is an easy sin to condemn in others. Jesus knew that this pageant was a deliberate trap. He knew the law said both parties were to be stoned; so where was the man? But notice how compassionate and forgiving Jesus was to both the woman and the shrewd Pharisees. After the woman was dragged through the dry and dusty street, manhandled, half-dressed, and thrown down at His feet, Jesus didn't mutter a word of condemnation to the woman. He just wrote each of her accuser's sins in the dust, starting with the oldest, so each one would know He read their hearts and minds. If I had that kind of information, I could imagine listing off every sin those Pharisees ever committed, from birth on, publishing it all on the front page of the *Jerusalem Times*, in bold colored print, and joyfully humiliating each one of those hypocrites. What they did to that woman is as low as a person can go. They weren't the bottom of the barrel; they were below the barrel, and just about unforgivable—but not to Jesus. Jesus didn't even expose them to their peers, much less the *Times*. He didn't embarrass any of His sinful children. He didn't condone what the woman did, nor did He embarrass her in front of the gathered crowd, but said, "I do not condemn you. Go and leave your life of sin."

How is that for forgiveness? The woman didn't even ask for forgiveness, and Jesus gave it anyway. Moreover, Jesus offered the Pharisees more compassion and forgiveness than He did the woman, for their sins were much worse than hers. What Jesus demonstrated is great news. It doesn't matter how badly you or I have acted or what skeletons are in our closet, God would never embarrass us. We may have some private sessions from time to time to discuss our former issues, but God will not unnecessarily point out our flaws publicly. Like the lost boy parable, He will cover us with His spotless robe. Think of all the sinners in the Bible: David, Rahab, Sampson, and others who have done some pretty bad things in their lives. God knows all that was done, including their motives, but He will never bring them up—and neither should we. God protects our reputations.

***

Some days I'm very tolerant. They usually come after enjoying a long night of dreamless sleep in a warm, soft bed, leisurely enjoying a gourmet breakfast that includes a fluffy omelet, fried potatoes that are salted just right, ice-cold fresh-squeezed orange juice, a steamy mug of hot chocolate, an hour of peaceful reading, and knowing I don't have an action-packed agenda. But, any other day may not produce the same fruits of the Spirit. When things are good, I'm nice. When things go bad, I may not be as loving. In contrast, look how Jesus acted after nearly dying in Gethsemane, enduring seven mock trials and a sleepless night, all after having Judas turn Him over to the police, and one of His best friends, Peter, deny that he even knew Him. Notice, too, how He acts and what He says after being beaten and whipped over and over, spat upon, and insulted, and all this without a breakfast. This is how God acts, not me. At least I would never have acted like that had I never seen His example.

> As the soldiers led him away, they seized Simon from Cyrene, who was on his way in from the country, and put the cross on him and made him carry it behind Jesus. A

lanber of people followed him, including women
wlrned and wailed for him.

Jened and said to them, "Daughters of Jerusalem,
dceep for me; weep for yourselves and for your
ch For the time will come when you will say,
'Bre the childless women, the wombs that never
bc the breasts that never nursed!' Then "they
wto the mountains, 'Fall on us!' and to the
hiver us!' For if people do these things when the
treen, what will happen when it is dry?" (Luke
2:1)

Tr men, both criminals, were also led out with
hi executed. When they came to the place called
tll, they crucified him there, along with the
cr—one on his right, the other on his left. Jesus
s*ther, forgive them, for they do not know what they
ar*" And they divided up his clothes by casting
lce 23:32–34)

Can yve that after being abused over and over, Jesus could say
to His en'Father, forgive them, for they do not know what they
are doing't Jesus show that He is the definition of forgiveness?
When His to forgive not seven times, but seventy times seven,
He was ong us to forgive as He forgives us.

Is God Severe?

When I ask people if they thought Jesus was ever severe, only one story is mentioned: the cleansing of the temple. Jesus cleansed the temple two times, first at the beginning of His ministry (John 2) and again at the end of His ministry after riding into Jerusalem on a young donkey. The story is found in Matthew 21.

> Jesus entered the temple courts and drove out all who were buying and selling there. He overturned the tables of the money changers and the benches of those selling doves. "It is written," he said to them, "'My house will be called a house of prayer,' but you are making it 'a den of robbers.'" The blind and the lame came to him at the temple, and he healed them. But when the chief priests and the teachers of the law saw the wonderful things he did and the children shouting in the temple courts, "Hosanna to the Son of David," they were indignant. "Do you hear what these children are saying?" they asked him. "Yes," replied Jesus, "have you never read, "'From the lips of children and infants you, Lord, have called forth your praise'?" And he left them and went out of the city to Bethany, where he spent the night. (Matt. 21:12–17)

What would it be like to be in a sunny, hot, church courtyard with small wooden handmade carts and brightly colored booths scattered around the entrance; people buying and selling lambs, oxen, sheep, goats, and birds by the score; merchants arguing about the price; money clinking; and children scurrying around? Then have someone come in and overthrow the carts and booths in such a manner that only the owners of the booths were afraid and not the children? You'll notice in the story the blind and lame stayed around too, and the children shouted, "Hosanna, to the Son of David." It seems to me that whatever Jesus really said and did was said and done in such a manner that only those who knew they were in the wrong felt the fear. As a child I knew that when my brother or sister was in trouble, and I was innocent, I didn't have to worry about my parents' anger or punishment. It is the same thing. In a very firm manner, Jesus turned the tables over because they were not supposed to be there polluting the temple court. They were making His Father's house of prayer into a noisy grocery store, and people were being lost because of it, but the innocent children knew He was not to be feared.

Was Jesus severe when James and John wanted to be first and second in the kingdom (Matt. 20:20–24)? Was Jesus severe when Peter denied knowing Him (Matt. 26:69–74), or when He healed the man at the Pool of Bethesda and suggested that he stop sinning lest a worse thing come upon him (John 5:1–14)? No. Was Jesus severe when He took the abuse from Pilot (Matt. 27)? Was Jesus retaliatory or severe when Judas met him in the garden with a kiss (Matt. 26:47–56)? Was Jesus severe when they spit in his face and struck him with their fists? Did Jesus ever retaliate? When you read the life and teachings of Jesus, you can look high and low, but you will not find an event where Jesus was arbitrary, exacting, unforgiving, or severe. On the contrary, Jesus showed that God is logical and reasonable, yielding and flexible, kind and gentle. He is forgiveness personified, and someone you would like to take home for dinner, someone you would cherish as a friend. Only when He needed to did He raise His voice, and when He did, He did it with love, truth, and a tear in His eye.

CHAPTER 29

Did Jesus Explain the Sinner's Death?

O ur death is an important topic. It doesn't matter whether we are talking about our first death or what the Bible calls the second death, most people don't want to talk about it. We would rather discuss the weather. I have tried to highlight some of the instances where people have had to die: Adam and Eve died after living 930 years, Cain killed Abel, God destroyed the Earth's entire population with the exception of Noah and his family, God rained fire and brimstone upon Sodom and Gomorrah, and God turned Lot's wife into a pillar of salt. Killing seemed to be just part of the narrative. God killed the firstborn of Egypt; the Israelites killed all the inhabitants of Canaan, and on and on. Do any of these deaths answer the question raised in the beginning? Does sin cause death? Or Does God kill sinners? Has the question been cleared up? Did Jesus ever directly address the accusation that God had lied about sin causing death? Yes, but not in a lecture. Because of the issue's complexity and because He had been accused of lying already, He chose instead to demonstrate it. The transfiguration, Gethsemane, and the cross all speak to the issue.

Transfiguration

Toward the end of His ministry, Jesus is transfigured (Matt. 17:1–13). Why? Jesus is allowed to talk to both Moses and Elijah for encouragement, but why the transfiguration? Was it so the disciples would be encouraged too, or is there more? Remember in Exodus, when Moses asked to see God's glory, God told him that no one can see His face and live, but in this story, Jesus is brought into the very presence of God, sees more than just God's backside, and He is unhurt. He lived thirty-three and a half years among the degenerate people on Earth and then stood in the Glory of God unscathed. Why is this important? God needed to answer one of Satan's claims: God's requirements were too hard for either angels or humans to live up to (Job 2:3-4). Christ revealed His purity by standing in God's presence unharmed. In fact, He reflected the image perfectly and radiated the same glory He had in the beginning with the Father. Christ showed He was sinless; His relationship with the Father was unbroken, even though He communed here on this dark planet and was dogged by Satan His entire life. Remember Jesus's temptations in the desert: forty days He fasted, for almost six weeks Jesus didn't eat, and He was assailed by Satan like no other being—ever. Jesus met Satan and his enticements head-on and gained the victory under incredibly difficult circumstances, much more severe than the circumstances under which Adam and Eve succumbed. Jesus demonstrated that men were not created defective, that the requirements of God could be met even under the most forbidding circumstances, and the glory of the Lord, His radiance—the fire associated with His presence—is not inherently dangerous but is life to those in harmony with God. The fire does not consume those who are pure.

> The sinners in Zion are terrified; trembling grips the godless: *"Who of us can dwell with the consuming fire? Who of us can dwell with everlasting burning?" He who walks righteously and speaks what is right,* who rejects gain from extortion and keeps his hand from accepting bribes, who

stops his ears against plots of murder and shuts his eyes against contemplating evil—this is the man who will dwell on the heights, whose refuge will be the mountain fortress. His bread will be supplied, and water will not fail him. (Isa. 33:14–15)

So with the transfiguration we learn that in the judgment, it isn't merely the fire that kills us. Christ lived in the flames, so if you are pure, God's presence is not in itself harmful. The fire is just God's glory, His majestic presence.

His body was like chrysolite, his face like lightning, his eyes like flaming torches, his arms and legs like the gleam of burnished bronze, and his voice like the sound of a multitude. (Dan. 10:6)

He made darkness his canopy around him—the dark rain clouds of the sky. *Out of the brightness of his presence bolts of lightning blazed forth*. The Lord thundered from heaven; the voice of the Most High resounded. (2 Sam. 22:12–14)

I looked, and I saw a windstorm coming out of the north—an immense cloud with flashing lightning and surrounded by brilliant light. The center of the fire looked like glowing metal, and in the fire was what looked like four living creatures. In appearance their form was that of a man. (Ezek. 1:4–5)

Until the appearing of our Lord Jesus Christ, which God will bring about in His own time—God, the blessed and only Ruler, the King of kings and Lord of lords, who alone is immortal and who lives in *unapproachable light*, whom no one has seen or can see. (1 Tim. 6:14–16)

These images and explanations of the light that surrounds our glorious God have been misused in many explanations of "hell." God's presence is surrounded with brilliant fire-like light, and God will be there in the judgment, but that does not mean we have to fear Him or His glory. Jesus showed us there is nothing to be afraid of in God's presence.

Gethsemane

They slept. One of the greatest events ever witnessed in the universe, and the disciples slept. It was finally time to do what the prophets foretold. It was time for Jesus to answer the questions, time to rescue us, and time to give us the reasons for our faith. For this incomparable event only three disciples were close enough to watch, and even then, they didn't see and hear all that followed, because they slept.

After leaving the Upper Room and their Passover meal, Jesus sorrowfully led His disciples out to the garden of Gethsemane to a place they had often come to pray. It was different this night though, like the eerie calm before a Kansas tornado strikes. The disciples could feel something ominous coming. What was it?

> Leaving the others, Jesus took Peter, James, and John further into the garden, and not wanting them to see the intense pain He was to endure, Jesus spoke earnestly to the three, "My soul is overwhelmed with sorrow to the point of death. Stay here and keep watch with me." Going a little farther, He fell with His face to the ground and prayed, "My Father, if it is possible, may this cup be taken from me. Yet not what I will, but as you will," and He did this three times (Matt. 26:36–46).

> An angel from heaven appeared to Him and strengthened Him. And being in anguish, He prayed more earnestly, and His sweat was like drops of blood falling to the ground. (Luke 22:43–44)

111

Sorrowful to the point of death and sweating drops of blood—what is going on here? This isn't natural, or is it? Jesus said something about a cup. What is the cup?

> In the hand of the Lord is a *cup* full of foaming wine mixed with spices; he pours it out, and all the wicked of the Earth drink it down to its very dregs. (Ps. 75:8)

> Awake, awake! Rise up, O Jerusalem, you who have drunk from the hand of the Lord the *cup of his wrath,* you who have drained to its dregs the goblet that makes men stagger. (Isa. 51:17)

> This is what the Lord, the God of Israel, said to me: "Take from my hand this *cup filled with the wine of my wrath* and make all the nations to whom I send you drink it." (Jer. 25:15)

> A third angel followed them and said in a loud voice: "If anyone worships the beast and his image and receives his mark on the forehead or on the hand, he, too, *will drink of the wine of God's fury, which has been poured full strength into the cup of his wrath.* He will be tormented with burning sulfur in the presence of the holy angels and of the Lamb. And the smoke of their torment rises for ever and ever. There is no rest day or night for those who worship the beast and his image, or for anyone who receives the mark of his name." (Rev. 14:9–11)

Isn't the cup God's wrath? Isn't God pouring out His "wrath" on Jesus like He will do to us sinners? Isn't the cup what the universe has been waiting to see?

Jesus was said to be sin, though He knew no sin; that He would save the world from its sins; and that by His stripes we would be healed. If you want to know what God does to the worst of the worst of sinners, shouldn't we look at what God did to Jesus? Shouldn't we study what happened when Jesus drank from the cup? What happened? He was given up. There in the garden, Jesus experienced the separation from the Father that comes from being let go as a sinner. As His unity with the Father broke up, His agony was too great to bear. Jesus fell to the earth and would have died right there had not an angel strengthened Him. The angel was an added measure; God had more for Jesus to show later and sent an angel to help Him through this near-death experience in Gethsemane. Without the angel's help, Jesus would have died in the garden and never made it to the cross.

God's wrath; the cup; said to be sin, though He knew no sin; these phrases are important, but they have become clichés to many people. What does it mean that Jesus became sin? His body didn't change or shrivel up. Doesn't it mean that Jesus will be treated like a sinner though He never sinned?

In Genesis it says, "The day you eat thereof you will die," and in Romans it says, "The wages of sin is death," but what does that mean? In Leviticus, God set up the sanctuary service, which included a lamb, blood, and death, but why? Why is there always this pairing of sin with death?

Does it mean: if you reject God you will die, or does it mean, if you disobey God you will die?

Does it mean: sin kills you, or because you sin, God kills you?

Does it mean: this is a legal sacrifice, and God is punishing His Son so He won't have to kill you, or is it something else?

Think about it. Why is Jesus dying?

The Cross—The Answer

Jesus's torture and death on the cross is either the greatest or the most despicable event ever witnessed in the history of the universe, and like in Gethsemane most of the disciples were unavailable: only John saw what went on at the cross. It is the greatest event in that it reveals what

God is like as no other act could ever expose—the height and depth and breadth of a Father's love, willing to give everything for His children. It is despicable that men, made in God's image, could stoop so low as to murder their Maker in the most painful manner possible and then rush home to keep the rules He had given.

Strengthened by an angel (whom the Father sent), Christ repeats what He did in Gethsemane, only this time with His religious family playing a part. What happens? We see Jesus hunted by the pious religious leaders with clubs and swords, and they overtake Him in the garden at night. Through seven mock trials, these descendants of sin whip, beat, and torture their loving Creator. They bloody His body. They drag Him through the streets as though He was a thief. They attempt to destroy their God in the most inhumane way known to man at that time—crucifixion.

We see Jesus on the cross, and, as He is dying, He cries out, "My God, My God, why have You forsaken me?" (Similar to Hosea 11:8 and Ps. 22). God treated Him like a sinner. God gave Him up, and Jesus died. The Father was there hiding in the shadows, crying, silently watching, as Jesus died that lonely death.

This was not a ceremony designed to propitiate the Father's anger. This was not a ritual designed to expiate the Father's wrath. This was not a sacrifice designed to instill forgiveness in the Father's heart for His fallen children. This was not a ransom payment to the Devil, to angels, or to sin. This was not a legal transaction paying off the Father or the Holy Spirit so they could forgive. It was a demonstration of truth, a demonstration of what God is like, a demonstration that would break our hearts and lead us home, a demonstration revealing what God does to sinners, a demonstration designed to answer the questions raised in heaven, a demonstration calculated to bring God and His creatures back together—forever—a true atonement. It was a demonstration clarifying what He told Satan and Adam and Eve in the beginning—if you sin you will die—and this is how I'm involved.

Jesus said to those gathered there, "Father, forgive them; they don't know what they are doing" (Luke 23:34). If Christ is willing to forgive even in these horrid circumstances, isn't God the Father also willing to forgive (John 10:30, 14:9)? But forgiveness isn't the problem, God loves to forgive, it is our paranoid fear of Him, and Jesus's life and death is supposed to remedy the situation.

> He who believes in the Son has everlasting life; and he who does not believe the Son shall not see life, but the wrath of God abides on him." (John 3:36, NKJV)

> Most assuredly, I say to you, he who hears My word and believes in Him who sent Me has everlasting life, and shall not come into judgment, but has passed from death into life. (John 5:24, NKJV)

> He who believes and is baptized will be saved; but he who does not believe will be condemned. (Mark 16:16, NKJV)

Christ was not telling the people something new; He was revealing to them what had always been true. God's attitude toward us has always been one of indescribable love and forgiveness. We were the ones to run from the relationship. We accepted Satan's lie that God could not be trusted. God was doing everything He could, in the most dramatic way He could, and in a way we could understand, to reveal the truth to us and the onlooking universe.

Ironically, those who should have been first to accept Him were the ones crying out for His death. The people whom God worked with for so long to stop worshiping idols were the ones clamoring for their Creator's blood. Was God proving something again to the angels and unfallen worlds? God would say, "Yes. This is what I wanted to tell you. This is what would have happened in heaven if I had allowed the natural consequences to occur with Satan before you were ready to see it. Satan's death would have scared you. Then you would have obeyed Me out of fear, and eventually, even if it took hundreds or thousands of years to develop, you would become like these first-century Jews. If you were to obey Me out of fear of punishment, fear of retribution, or fear of vengeance, merely to obtain a reward—or for any other motive short of understanding love and friendship—eventually, though outwardly loyal, you would treat Me just as these Jewish leaders did and try to put Me to death. Like them you would have honored me with your lips, but your hearts would be far from Me; you would look loyal on the outside but hate Me on the inside; you would look clean on the outside but inside be full of dead men's bones. I do not want our relationship to be that of a servant to a king, because servants will eventually hate and kill their master. I need you to love Me and be My friends. I need you to understand these issues, because if you don't understand, and you do things merely by rote, you will eventually become like these Jewish leaders.

Had I not taken the long route to explain sin and death and what I am really like, you and My entire universe would be baying for My blood. There are no shortcuts to what I really want in My universe. I want love, respect, freedom of choice, and freedom from fear for all my creatures, and I would rather die Myself than sacrifice these values. Paul states the ultimate purpose of Christ's death in Romans 3:25–26:

> Whom God set forth *as* a propitiation by His blood, through faith, *to demonstrate His righteousness,* because in His forbearance God had passed over the sins that were previously committed, *to demonstrate at the present time His righteousness,* that He might be just and the justifier of the one who has faith in Jesus. (NKJV)

> Paul could not have stated more emphatically that the *purpose of the cross was to demonstrate the truth about God's own character,* the truth that is the basis of our friendship and trust. God considers all those who trust Him enough to listen and obey to be righteous, set right, good, justified, savable. (Maxwell 1992)

Why is it necessary to understand that God is not an executioner? Because, servants who are afraid of God's potential punishment will not stay servants forever; they will become his enemies someday, even if they look good in church and in the community for the time being. Who cried out for Christ's death? Was it the heathen Romans? No. The Romans were more kind and compassionate than the Jews, the followers of God. Is it any wonder that today the secular and nonchurched can be nicer people than those who go to church and have a harsh picture of God? Those who demanded the life of the Son were the most conscientious churchgoers that have ever lived on the planet, and what good did it do them?

It is a dreadful thought, but those who killed Christ may be a lot like you and me. They believed in God the Creator and revered His authority and power. They believed in the Bible and read it all of the time. They accepted all Ten Commandments and even added a few. They supported the church by paying tithe. They ate nothing that was forbidden. And they kept themselves and their children separate from unbelievers by supporting church schools instead of the local public schools. Does this sound like anyone you know? It sounds like me. I'm not suggesting we shouldn't do good things or keep the rules, but there are some striking similarities. The problem is they never internalized the rules or looked at the logic supporting their presuppositions. Do we? They didn't ask why these things needed to be—they just did what they were told by the leading pastors and teachers of the day. They looked like good obedient servants, but they were not His friends. They completely missed the point of why God gave the sacrifices, and, therefore, why Jesus had to die. They even thought Jesus was possessed by demons and had the devil's picture of God (John 7:20).

Do you remember the section in Micah 6 which began with the rhetorical question: "With what shall I come before the Lord?" Micah replies, "Shall I come before Him with burnt offerings, with calves a year old? Will the Lord be pleased with thousands of rams, with ten thousands of rivers of oil? Shall I give my firstborn for my transgression, the fruit of my body for the sin of my soul?" Though it isn't written, the rhetorical answer is no. No, God is not really interested in my attempts to pacify Him with offerings or sacrifices; no, sacrifices are not what He really wants. He wants mutual trust, love, humility, a willingness to listen to Him and do what is right—He wants our faith; but yes,

God has requested that we offer sacrifices, because there was a lesson in it for us, not an appeasement in it for Him. Do you think this passage just refers to the blood of lambs and bulls and goats in Micah's day? Do you think this might also be applied to us today and Jesus's sacrifice? Did God just need better blood than that of rams, lambs, and doves to be appeased? Will God feel like He can forgive you and me only if He gives His *Firstborn* for my transgression, the *Fruit of His body* for the sin of my soul? What do you think?

The first-century Jews believed the text: "That without the shedding of blood there could be no forgiveness of sins" (Heb. 9:22), and they killed thousands and thousands of animals proving it. Jesus's blood was shed, and it was the right blood, but it didn't do them any good because it didn't bring them to a new relationship with God, a relationship characterized by faith. They really didn't understand that the ceremonies, the laws, the sacrifices, and especially Jesus's death, were all designed to lead them to a passionate love for Christ, who said, "If you have seen Me you have seen the Father."

It was difficult for God to demonstrate what happens to sinners, because Christ was not a sinner. He was made to be sin, but He never sinned, so Christ couldn't really die like a sinner does in God's presence. If Jesus had sinned, it would have been easy. He would have perished in the transfiguration event when exposed to God's glory. But He had never separated Himself from the Father.

The transfiguration, Gethsemane, and the cross taken together help us understand the judgment. The transfiguration showed God's glory— the "fire" is not harmful to His faithful creatures; we can live in the splendor of His presence. Gethsemane shows that sinners do really die, and it isn't God killing them in anger, but sadly letting them go, letting them suffer the natural consequences of their choices. Combining the two thoughts, in the judgment, it won't be God arbitrarily saving some and killing others, but when He does reveal Himself, some will live, some will die, and as Jesus demonstrated, it won't be an enjoyable experience for the lost. The cross reinforced what we saw in Gethsemane and showed us what can happen to people and angels who have a false concept of what God is like and have grown to fear Him. Even though they look "loyal" for a time, fearful people, if given a chance, will kill their kind and gentle Creator.

The Resurrection

Although the legal separation of the thirteen American colonies from Great Britain was proposed on June 7, 1776, it actually occurred on

July 2, 1776, when the Second Continental Congress voted to secede, and it wasn't until two days later, July 4, that Congress approved the wording of the Declaration of Independence and had it published. That is why July 4, and not June 7 or July 2, is the day Americans remember their independence—that is when the good news got out. And now, every year on the Fourth of July, American's burn up more than twenty thousand tons of fireworks celebrating the event.

What would it mean if we were to celebrate our independence on May 5 (Cinco de Mayo), or December 25 (Christmas), or September 11 (the day New York's World Trade Center towers were destroyed)? Would it make any difference? In a similar manner, though Jesus was crucified on Passover Friday (which is significant), and rested in the tomb during the Sabbath hours (which is also significant), we associate Christ's entire life and death with the day Jesus rose from the tomb—Sunday. What difference would there be if Christ had been resurrected on Friday night or on the Sabbath, or even on Monday? Why didn't He rise from the dead a year later? Why was there a resurrection at all?

In several places Jesus comments on His future resurrection saying: "I am the resurrection and the life. He who believes in me will live, even though he dies" (John 11:25). And in Mark 9:31, Jesus said, "The Son of Man is going to be betrayed into the hands of men. They will kill Him, and after three days He will rise." Later, Paul talks about the resurrection in Romans 6:5, "If we have been united with him like this in his death, we will certainly also be united with him in his resurrection." Knowing we will see our Savior again is awesome news, but notice, it doesn't explain why He was resurrected on Sunday morning and not some other day. Why did Jesus die and rise up a day and a half later? Was it just to fulfill prophesy? What should it say to us and the onlooking universe?

What would God be saying to us if Jesus had been resurrected on Friday afternoon, within hours of having his side pierced? What if He had risen from the tomb, walked back into the city, back into the temple, and shown the people and the rulers who had clamored for His death that He did have power over the grave—that He was the Messiah. Jesus's very presence would have leveled the place and caused a riot. It would have certainly showed Jesus had told the truth and that He was God. But this act would have counteracted what He had worked so hard to achieve: that God wants to be worshiped because of His beautiful character, not because of His power or ability to perform miracles. If Christ were to rise up immediately after being killed and show Himself publicly, the gospel would have gone to the world in weeks, if not days, but what gospel would be going out? Would the people have been converted, having new hearts and minds? Would they now love the Lord with all their heart and mind and strength and their neighbors as themselves? No, the good news—what God is really like—would have become merely the gospel of the miraculous, which is, by the way, what most people in the world are still looking for.

What would have been revealed if Christ had risen on Saturday? First, coming back to life on Sabbath morning, only sixteen hours later, would not have given the people very much time to contemplate the importance of His death. Second, we wouldn't have Jesus resting in the tomb giving the Sabbath more significance. If Jesus isn't respecting the day anymore, why should anyone else? Having Jesus resurrected on Saturday would have radically eroded the significance of the Ten Commandments.

What would we have learned if Jesus had been resurrected on Monday, three days later? Tradition taught that a person's "soul" hovered near a dead person for three days, so staying dead for at least three days would prove to all the skeptics that Jesus really did die, and that is why Jesus waited four days before resurrecting Lazarus. But Jesus's death had already been proven when a soldier ran Him through with his blade, and blood and water poured out of His body (John 19:34). A Monday resurrection does not prove that Jesus really did die or add any significance to the event. What would a Tuesday, Wednesday, or Thursday resurrection say in addition to what God had already stated? What more information would we gather if Jesus had been resurrected a week, a month, or even a year later on the next Passover? Nothing.

With an eye bent toward the question, was Jesus's death a legal sacrifice? What would it say if Jesus had stayed in the tomb? What would it say if Jesus was never resurrected? That would suggest there was a real legal exchange for our salvation. If the wages of sin is a forever-death and not just a death, sleep, and quick resurrection, and if Jesus died that forever-death for us and was still in the tomb today, then legally we could say He paid the debt. But Jesus's Sunday resurrection negates that concept and declares that God did not need to have a legal payment to forgive our sins. The resurrection affirms that God is not a legalist. Jesus's death was a demonstration, showing us and the universe the true consequences of sin and what God meant when He said, "The wages of sin is death."

Chapter 30

Two More Demonstrations

Jesus said He would come back soon, and it is alluded to many times throughout scripture. Second to faith, Jesus's return, and the events surrounding it, is the most talked about teaching in the New Testament. And for me it is way overdue. Like you, I want to see all of God's promises come true. I want to see Jesus, God the Father, Holy Spirit, and all the angels break through the darkness of our pitch-black planet and make all things new again. I want to sip from the crystal-clear river and savor the twelve fruits that fall from the Tree of Life. I want to soar like an eagle, and run and not be weary. I want to see my family with the healthy glow of eternity in their eyes and faces in a place where there are no more tears or sadness, where Satan and evil and ghettos and death are no more. I want to eat the leaves from that tree which bring healing to the nations. I want to see the city whose maker is God and where sickness and suffering are only known from history books. And pain—all the pain from the accumulated millennia: the wars, the disease, the child abuse, the maimed and broken bodies of people in wheelchairs, and the pain from unmet expectations, and the pain from broken homes and broken backs and broken hearts, is gone. I want Jesus to come back because I want to meet Him and see what love looks like in a face. I want to hear His words and not merely read them; I want to hear the sound of music, love, acceptance, and peace

124

intertwined. I want to meet the angels who have been cheering us on, and travel from planet to planet and galaxy to galaxy learning the secrets of science. I want to learn about chemistry and physics and music from the one whose knowledge is infinite, unborrowed, and underived.

But most of all, I want to see God the Father. I want to talk to Him, knowing that He chose me long before I chose Him. He knew my name before the foundation of the world and what I'd become. Knowing what poor choices I would make, He was still willing to watch over me, and love me and my family and friends. I want to tell Him I love Him and appreciated the fact that, though others have, He never left me or forsook me and that He was always there to listen and help when I was at my last thread. And because of what Jesus has shown me, I'm not afraid, and I know that I can actually bring Him some joy, too, like my family brings me joy. Just thinking about them brings a smile to my face, and I know I can bring a smile to God's face too, when He thinks of me. And I know that He's happy when He thinks of you, too.

So where is He? What is He waiting for? Why hasn't He come back to gather His children together? He said it was finished at the cross, so what else could He possibly need to prove? Revelation chapters six and seven give us a clue. They tell of Jesus's second coming and ask a stunning question:

> I watched as he opened the sixth seal. There was a great earthquake. The sun turned black like sackcloth made of goat hair, the whole moon turned blood red, and the stars in the sky fell to earth, as figs drop from a fig tree when shaken by a strong wind. The heavens receded like a scroll being rolled up, and every mountain and island was removed from its place. Then the kings of the earth, the princes, the generals, the rich, the mighty, and everyone else, both slave and free, hid in caves and among the rocks of the mountains. They called to the mountains and the rocks, "Fall on us and hide us from the face of him who sits on the throne and from the

wrath of the Lamb! For the great day of their wrath has come, *and who can withstand it?"* (Rev. 12:6–17)

Christ's coming sounds ominous, doesn't it? But it doesn't need to; we know what God's wrath is. And who can withstand it? Chapter 7 tells us:

> After this I saw four angels standing at the four corners of the earth, holding back the four winds of the earth to prevent any wind from blowing on the land or on the sea or on any tree. Then I saw another angel coming up from the east, having the seal of the living God. He called out in a loud voice to the four angels who had been given power to harm the land and the sea: "Do not harm the land or the sea or the trees until we put a seal on the foreheads of the servants of our God." Then I heard the number of those who were sealed: 144,000 from all the tribes of Israel.

> After this I looked, and there before me was a great multitude that no one could count, from every nation, tribe, people and language, standing before the throne and before the Lamb. They were wearing white robes and were holding palm branches in their hands. (Rev. 7:1–4, 9–10)

Two groups of people will be present when Christ comes back: those who have bought the devil's picture of God and who are afraid of God and his coming, and a multitude of God's faithful friends who are sealed into the truth of what God is like. God is waiting for His children to grow up, become mature, and become so sealed that they cannot be moved though they are tried to the uttermost.

Taking the broadest possible perspective, God will demonstrate that the truth and the light and the good news that He has presented works. Countless hours and resources have been expended since creation. Has it been worth it? Has the war been won in the minds of angels and men?

What the angels in heaven could not do, poor, weak, fallen, and sinful humanity will do. The angels did not know God well enough in the beginning and were deceived by Satan into thinking that God could give arbitrary laws with arbitrary and exacting punishments; that He plays favorites and could be severe and could lie to His creatures; that He could torture them and even kill them if they sinned. Because God values personal freedom above everything, Satan was allowed the freedom to do and say anything to the angels that he could conceive. He was allowed to paint his case against God as black as tar, and He will be allowed to do it again; only this time, humanity will not fail like the angels did. After all the evidence has been presented, after the history of how God treated Israel and the nations, and after the truth was revealed in Gethsemane and the cross, God's friends will stand true, knowing the truth, and will not be deceived by Satan's lies.

In this showdown, as with Job, Satan will be allowed to do anything he likes except take our lives. Though tried to the uttermost with signs, lies, and wonders, the remnant will not let God down like Adam and Eve did. They will not lose their faith in what God is like; they will not join the side of Satan and rebel like Korah or trade sides like Judas. God will demonstrate that we mortals are safe to save, and our neighbors in heaven have a right to know that rebellion will not rise up twice.

And to be that kind of person is no small thing. It isn't just asking for forgiveness and becoming "saved." Being saved is great, but that is not going to be enough to cut the mustard at this crucial time in history. God will need people who know and love the truth like Job and Moses and Daniel and Joseph. Are you that person? Maybe not today, but what about in a year? Will you try?

In the beginning, God did not allow the natural consequence of Lucifer's rebellion to take place because those looking on would not have understood that it wasn't God destroying Lucifer (we covered that already); they would have feared God and rebelled. The angels got that message at the cross—we didn't. Now, God is waiting for us to get the same message. God will wait until His people understand the issues in the Great Controversy and the meaning of His "wrath." He will wait until the planet has been warned about the seven last plagues, the plagues that occur when God finally gives up our planet to Satan's control.

God will wait until the world knows the destruction of the wicked is just the natural consequence of their choices, not His anger. He will not allow people to see these terrifying events and think He is causing it. If He came too soon and people witnessed those awesome events unprepared, they would fear Him in the future, and that would threaten the peace and harmony of the next life. God is waiting for us to understand that the destruction we will see in the end is not Him destroying His disobedient children.

And, wouldn't it be just like God to demonstrate that what He has done in humanity has actually worked before bringing us to heaven? Do you think the angels might have questions regarding their future "fallen" neighbors? I do. I believe God is going to demonstrate that weak, imperfect past sinners—those who lived after what was demonstrated by God throughout the centuries—can be totally healed, can stay true to God, and not let Him down, even though Satan is free to do anything he wants to do except take our lives.

The last demonstration will be one thousand years after the second coming, after the resurrection of the wicked, during the period we call the Judgment. Why would a God of indescribable love resurrect those who were not going to heaven? Wouldn't it be cruel to make so many people die twice, to burn those who lived in Sodom and Gomorrah two times? Wouldn't it be good enough that they just stay dead, or does God have to somehow even the score? Maybe God really does, in the end, live by an eye-for-an-eye and a tooth-for-a-tooth. Do sinners really have to "pay" for their sins?

Consider this. God has put to "sleep" millions of His children in various ways, sons and daughters that may not have been evil. God killed the firstborn in Egypt, but were all of those children wicked? God killed 185,000 Assyrians in one swipe, but were they all coldhearted and evil? God killed forty children with bears, and did they die as hardened, unrepentant sinners? No. They were collateral damage. God chose to do those things for other reasons. But who is to say if they should be saved or lost? Might it be said that God wasn't fair?

And what about those who knew not the God of Israel: the Mayan, Incas, Mongols, American Indians, Vikings, and Eskimos? Are they lost because they were born in a different place and time? A close investigation is needed, and to answer the question, or better yet, demonstrate it, God will raise all from the grave and show them the truth about their lives. Then each person will demonstrate his or her response to this truth when God reveals His glory. Now, because we have seen Jesus's death, we won't misunderstand what is going on. All the people that have ever been born and all the angels ever created will be present. Both good and bad will witness the next event. As God reveals His glory, the glory He has shrouded ever since Satan rebelled in the beginning, we will see God as He really is, in His fullest glory, and those who are in harmony with Him will rejoice and thrive in the splendor, like when Jesus was transfigured, but the others will sadly perish. Is God killing His rebellious children? No. They are reaping the natural consequences of their choices (Isa. 33). They have personally thrown their eternal life away. At this point it is possible for some to live longer in God's fiery presence than others, but it won't be God supernaturally keeping some alive as torture; instead, it will be the natural course of events. In the end, God pronounces the choices that we have made: "He that is unjust let him be unjust still; he that is filthy, let him be filthy still; he that is righteous, let him be righteous still; he that is holy, let him be holy still" (Rev. 22:11). Jesus said that He doesn't judge; Moses does. In other words, how have you and I responded to the truth (John 5:45)? Jesus also said, "I judge no man" (John 8:15). The last demonstration will reveal the truth, that with even greater light, those outside the city's gates are incurable and unsavable. There is nothing more God could have done to save them.

Part 2

Train Wrecks

CHAPTER 31

Three Train Wrecks

You will find this next section to be much different in style. In story form or parable, the traditional version and the Great Controversy-Demonstration version of why Jesus had to die are compared and contrasted. It helps to look at concepts from varying perspectives. Sometimes, if a theory is placed in a different setting, then the contrasts are greater and easier to see. These stories are about trains. One train is located out in space on some unidentified planet, and two others are in good ol' Kansas. The forth story comes straight from Satan himself, and the last story highlights the traditional atonement theology.

The *Star Wars* Train Wreck: A long time ago in a galaxy far, far away, there was a train tearing down a set of tracks through a long, dark tunnel. The train blazed near light speed yet was invisible. It was powerful and sinister, and seemed to hiss silently as it sinuously slid through the S-shaped curves of the mountain like a serpent. I watched as it exited the tunnel just a half-mile north of the Emerald City—the city whose citizens, up to this point, didn't know that this train even existed, though its tracks had been part of the landscape for as long as any of them could remember. These peaceful people were ruled over by a benevolent father and one of his many sons, Phosphorus, a brilliant young man who was intrigued with learning new things. Phosphorus wanted to investigate those train tracks and wanted to see where the tunnel led; he wanted to search out the unknown—go where no one had gone before. But his wise father warned him not to go, saying there was danger there, and insisted that if Phosphorus went down those tracks, he would die. Thinking his freedom was being restricted, he raced to the palace, and in a tirade accused his father of lying. In front of everyone he screamed: "If I die, it is because you are going to kill me. There's nothing down those tracks that will hurt me; in fact, you are probably withholding something wonderful, something awesome, something that'll make me great, maybe even greater than you!" And with that he bolted out of the palace and onto the tracks.

Meanwhile, the wise sage, knowing His son had spurned his advice, temporarily derailed the train using Jedi-like powers, so the boy wouldn't be killed. But now, because the young man hadn't immediately died, it looked like the sage had lied about the tracks leading to death, and the boy turned a large part of the city against his father, precipitating a dreadful war.

Then, many years later, "in the fullness of time," when He had the attention of all of the citizenry, the wise sage purposely, deliberately, lumbered down those tracks and into that long, dark tunnel, publicly, in view of his entire realm, and was smashed by the speeding train. He did this to prove that He was telling the truth, that He wasn't a liar, and that going down certain paths will naturally lead to death. This demonstration showed that the old sage hadn't lied, and thus brought an end to the war.

Earthly Train Wreck: A pretty young lady dressed in a cute pink dress wandered onto a set of rusty red steel train tracks near Maple Hill, Kansas—tracks that never seem to bend as they merge into a single black line, eventually pouring over the flat horizon. Fatigue leads her to sit down on the sun-drenched tracks. Being young, she doesn't understand what train tracks are for. Jesus yells out from a small hill overlooking the tracks: "Get off the tracks or you will die! There is something you don't understand." But, she doesn't know Him or trust Him and stays on the tracks. He sends people to tell her she's in danger, but she doesn't trust them either, and the train rises over the horizon. Then, in a desperate move, just in the nick of time, Jesus leaps onto the tracks, pushes her out of the way, and is killed by the collision with the train. After He is resurrected, He says, "Now, if you trust Me, you can go back with Me to heaven."

Was it a legal swap or some kind of payment? Not really. Did He tell the truth about the train? Yes. Did He die for her? Yes, but not in the usual sense of the term. Did she learn the lesson? Hopefully, yes. Now she will trust Jesus in the future and won't go down that track. Is anyone going to say she got off too easily or the consequences were too light? No! It cost the Creator His life to demonstrate the truth.

Traditional Train Wreck: Again, a pretty young lady dressed in a light pink dress is wondering down a set of rusty red steel train tracks. Again, she is oblivious to the purpose of train tracks and to her ignorant condition. God yells out, "Get off the tracks, or I will have to punish you! The wages for standing on train tracks is death." And because she is on the "forbidden tracks," God sends a train out of the train yard to punish her. God continues, "I have a law that says, if you step on the tracks, you must die. In fact, if you even think about standing on the train tracks in your heart, you must die." She disobeys and remains on the tracks, so God sends people to tell her how bad she is, that she's in big trouble for disobeying Him, and that she must repent. Then, again, just before the train's impact, just in the nick of time, Jesus shows up out of nowhere, shoves her off the tracks, and stands there gritting His teeth waiting for the train to strike, and is killed by the impact, suffering the death penalty for her.

After His resurrection, He says, "If you ask for forgiveness and believe I took your punishment—that is, I have vicariously paid the price of sin on your behalf—then you can come with Me back to heaven."

What do you think? These may not be the best analogies—they illustrate truth but are simplistic. In this case, sin and train tracks are synonymous; both take you places, but you may not like the final destination. And let me stress, I am not making light of anyone's beliefs, but I want to show the difference between what I consider the Great Controversy view (Trains No. 1 and No. 2) and the traditional view of the atonement (Train No. 3).

The traditional view generally restricts the meaning of Jesus's death to being merely something God required Jesus to do so He could legally forgive you and me.

The Great Controversy view has Jesus's death demonstrating the meaning of God's words, "the wages of sin is death," showing the natural consequences of sin (rebellion), and how God is involved in the death of the wicked.

Instead of a complex legal arrangement, the Bible is the history of how God has demonstrated His character after being accused by Satan as being an untrustworthy, unloving, lying God. And Jesus's death:

1. demonstrated that God didn't lie about sin causing death,
2. demonstrated that this death was not a vengeful act on God's part but rather the natural consequences of rebellious choices,
3. demonstrated God's loving character by showing us the truth first, Himself, before any of His creatures had to experience it,
4. demonstrated how low people can sink when they embrace a formal, legal, loveless religion, and
5. demonstrated what God's "wrath" is all about.

CHAPTER 32

———◦◦◦꧁◉꧂◦◦◦———

Satan's Train Wreck

I n Lucifer's mind he is the victim. He is the one who has had his character maligned. He is the one who has been accused of being a selfish, cruel, oppressive leader, and a liar about the results of sin. In his mind, all he wanted was to make the universe a better place, a place where everyone (especially him) could reach his or her greatest potential. From Lucifer's perspective he has been wrongly stripped of his authority, wrongly made to grovel at Christ's feet, and wrongly exiled from heaven, all because he had the gall to question God's authority. After some of the issues became public via either backyard gossip or head-to-head verbal clashes, Lucifer tried to "reason" with the angels and explain what it was really like working under God's "weak" leadership.

In Satan's words:

I didn't want to expose God's poorer characteristics. I tried to keep things covered up for as long as possible hoping to protect His reputation, but I couldn't do it any longer; the issues grew too big, too fast, and they had to be addressed. Like with Nixon's Watergate tapes, the events just unraveled. Then, in front of everyone, I was slandered and accused of lying. I was escorted to the throne room and ruthlessly interrogated. My integrity, my motives, and my loyalty were all drug through the mud. I was publicly humiliated! If you question God's wisdom one time, you are out. Challenge His authority or question His judgment, just one time, and you lose your position. God is covering up the truth with smoke and mirrors. God may say He loves, but the truth says otherwise.

Give me an impartial jury, give me just two or three other beings that haven't been bought off by God, and I know they will agree with me. It is God that is wrong. I'll prove it!

God created the earth and placed Adam, Eve, and me on it. God also placed two trees in the center of the garden, and I was confined to the Tree of Good and Evil, at least until the humans approached me. When Eve came close enough to talk, I told her my side of the story. "God's a pretty good guy," I said, "but He's holding out on you, Eve. You could be more, Eve, but God is withholding something wonderful, something awesome, something that will make you great, maybe even greater than He is. Trust me, I'm telling the truth." Then Eve cast her vote on my side, ate the fruit, and convinced Adam of the truth too.

I won! I won! The jury sided with me, I cried. I thought the controversy was over, but God didn't surrender. I protested. I won, but look, God won't admit it. And now look what He's done to Adam and Eve. After Adam and Eve's declaration that I was right, God kicked them out of the garden, took away the Tree of Life, pronounced a curse on the ground, and told the pair they would have to die. [Still gloating] I told you God was like that. Disobey one command, one time, and you get kicked out of the family; disgraced, you have to live on the street without even the necessities of life. He makes them break their backs with hard labor, and in the end, He kills them anyway. God, He's even worse than I thought. He really is arbitrary, exacting, unforgiving, and terribly severe. And He does kill those who won't obey Him in the end.

As the world became populated, not everyone wanted to obey God's every whim, so God sent a flood to destroy all those who have minds of their own, all those who could think and reason independently, all those that couldn't be paid off by God's "blessings." God killed millions in a destructive display of power. He drowned the men, the women, the children, the babies, and even their pets. I told you God was like that. Don't do it His way, have a mind of your own, and He'll kill you. Believe me, I have known God for what seems like an eternity, and although He may not show it often, God is terrifying if you don't obey Him to the letter. God shook and thundered at Mount Sinai and Mount Carmel, killed innocent young boys with bears, killed thousands of Assyrians, destroyed whole countries with plagues of flies, lice, hail, and frogs; and He killed the firstborn babies of Egypt. I told you God was like that. If you don't obey to a "T," He'll kick you out, starve you out, burn you out, flood you out, or even have you and your family stoned for breaking the Sabbath. That is what God is really like. And the coup de grâce: when Jesus came to Earth to show us what God was "really" like, He faked it. He never really came. It was all a mirage.

***

In Satan's version of the Train Wreck, there never was a real train or train tracks. There never was any shadowy evil that would mysteriously kill someone if they dared go that direction. It was all a façade. God used the threat of death to keep control over His creatures. He lied to keep them from gaining power, to hide His weaknesses, to obfuscate His arbitrary nature, to hold beings down and keep them subservient so He could feel all-powerful and puffed up. In Satan's version, God lied about sin causing death and cannot be trusted!

CHAPTER 33

The Traditional Train Wreck

The Traditional Train Track theology has been a great instrument to bring people into a saving relationship with Christ. For millennia this view of the gospel has saved souls, uplifting millions from the degradation of sin, and has given people hope in a future—immortal life with someone as loving as the Son. I am not attempting to belittle the billions of people who have come to love the Lord and have adopted this traditional view of the plan of salvation. I have believed this view. This is the view I learned when I first became a Christian, and I am thankful for it, but I have come to believe there is a better model.

Because the real biblical story is long and complicated, many Christians settle for a simpler version of the gospel to tell their church, parish, or children—an easier, quicker version, so the "babes in the truth" might grasp some of the love God has for them. We say simply, "Jesus loves you" or "Jesus died for you." In a similar fashion, because being saved is literally a life and death future reality, and because we all want everyone else to be saved; and you may only get one chance to tell someone the gospel, we tell people only the basics: "God is love; you are a sinner; Jesus paid the price; there's no other name given under heaven by which you can be saved; believe in Jesus Christ and you will be saved, and all those that believe and are baptized will be saved." But we don't always give the rest of the details; we don't always explain why those things are true, and they become clichés. Without the correct context, those phrases pick up meanings that are not accurate, and when taken collectively actually give a false picture of the Father.

Also, because many people are satisfied with a servant-like relationship with God, they don't look closely at the logic of ideas or ask questions when statements don't make sense. We accept conflicting ideas like: as a sinner you can't approach God on your own, because He is too holy, and you are not worthy; thus, you need a mediator, a go-between, Jesus, your High Priest. But then we find that Jesus is God too. We find that Jesus was the Rock who led Israel through the Wilderness (1 Cor. 10). So who had to mediate between Jesus and Judas; who had to mediate between Moses and God on Mount Sinai, and who had to mediate between Abraham and God when they were discussing Sodom and Gomorrah? Who had to mediate between the Old Testament high priest and God, while the high priest was mediating for the Israelites? No one. This conundrum, along with John 14:9 ("Anyone who has seen Me has seen the Father") and John 16:26 ("I say *not* unto you that I will pray the Father for you. No, the Father Himself loves you.") leads me to believe that God gave this imagery just to help people out at the very time they needed it most, and in this case, with help from a mediator, but God does not need for us to have a mediator—we do, because we are afraid. And along the same vein, God does not need a sacrifice to propitiate His wrath—we do, and for the same reason. We are afraid of God and feel better ourselves if we think He has been appeased. It reduces the fear. Moreover, how does this make sense? God cannot forgive one of His children for a sin without the death of His Son? Could you not forgive your daughter's lie without having your own son die? Are we more forgiving than God? I don't think so. There is a way to make sense of this, but not with the Traditional Train Wreck theology.

Because the traditional view of God has been made so high and exalted yet so mysterious in many churches, and it is obvious He can run His universe any way He wants, when we read or hear something that does not make sense, we are told, "just have faith, sister," or "we just can't understand God's indiscernible ways, brother." Because many churches teach that the Bible is too hard for the bewildered flock to understand, many people don't even try to make sense out of it. We let those with theology degrees tell us what it all means. And because the Traditional Train Wreck theology doesn't incorporate the book of Revelation with the war in heaven, some Christians have settled for a theology that may actually support the accusation that God is arbitrary, exacting, unforgiving, severe, and a liar about sin causing death, but wrap it up in colorful phrases of love and grace and forgiveness.

The Traditional Train Wreck Story

The Traditional Train Wreck goes like this: Our sovereign God created this world with Adam and Eve to rule it under His authority. But before He could trust them enough to let them rule, He had to test them; He had to see if they would obey. The test was simple: forbid them from eating a piece of fruit. But because they listened to Satan's suggestions, they disobeyed, ate the forbidden fruit, and failed the test. As part of their punishment for their first sin, they were ejected from the garden, banned from the life-perpetuating Tree of Life, and doomed to a life full of pain and suffering that would end in death. But there was more. Because of their sin, they would have to endure the second death, or eternal death, unless a substitute could be found to die for them.

The stories of God flooding the world, God killing the firstborn in Egypt, God killing the 185,000 Assyrians, the fire and brimstone of Sodom and Gomorrah, and the multitudinous rules, including the Ten Commandments, are all looked upon as a sovereign god's indisputable will being exercised on this planet as he corrects his disobedient and sometimes rebellious subjects. Eventually, though, in the fullness of time, God sends Jesus as a sacrifice, to "pay" for our sins and appease God's wrath, because the wages of sin is death (Rom. 6:23), and somebody had to pay for all those sins.

Let us consider this scenario. The fruit that God chose to forbid, was there a reason that God chose that tree, that piece of fruit? No, not in this scenario; it could have been any tree if God was just testing their obedience. So it was an arbitrary choice. God had to pick something to forbid, right? The definition of arbitrary is: something not planned or chosen for a particular reason; a demand not based on reason. God's choice of that tree, that fruit, that test, and that punishment was arbitrary. God was unnecessarily placing them into a position to fail.

In the Great Controversy Model, God counseled the inexperienced pair to stay away from the tree, away from eating of the fruit, because that was where Satan was constrained, and He knew Satan would lie to them there. It wasn't merely a test of their obedience. He was protecting them as much as He could and still allowing Satan an opportunity to tell his side of the story. It is true they did eat the fruit, but the damage had already been exacted—they had already taken Satan's side in the war. The fruit was really just a visual ballot box indicating which side they were on.

Don't eat that fruit, or I'll kick you out of your garden home is exacting. Not to make excuses for them, but Adam and Eve were relatively young, innocent, and naive. Making one mistake, disobeying by eating the wrong fruit, one time, and having to die for it, is severe. And if God couldn't forgive them, then He is unforgiving too. But most Christians take this text to the bank: the wages of sin is death, and believe God not only has the right but the obligation to put people to death for the smallest act of disobedience.

In the Great Controversy model, forgiveness is not really the problem. God did forgive them, but that didn't make everything right. Adam and Eve had sided with Satan, their concept of God had been damaged, and without a change in heart, without healing the relationship, the results eventually would be their death. The Traditional model assumes that forgiveness is all that we need, but that is wrong. Sin is worse than that; it requires healing the damage done, repairing the broken relationship, uniting the two estranged parties, and changing our views about God and His goodness. God sent them out of the garden and into an environment where they could see the results of sin and compare them to the garden—a living visual aid.

Now to be fair, the Traditional Train Wreck continues with a generous, gracious, and forgiving Son who will intercede with our stern

Father on our behalf. The Son will come and die an ignominious death, vicariously, to appease the Father's anger and wrath. And because of Jesus's earthly experience, He now knows what it is like to be tempted and can better judge the hearts of men than the Father. So, if you have faith in Jesus, and ask for forgiveness, you will be welcomed into heaven without having to experience hell.

This view falls short when you consider Jesus's statement: If you have seen Me, you have seen the Father (John 14:9). If Jesus loves us enough to experience life as a human, withstand the temptations and forty days of fasting in the wilderness, endure the experiences in the garden of Gethsemane and the cross, for us, then the Father would be willing to do the same. You cannot have one member of the Trinity willing to die and appease the other members of the Trinity's wrath and say, "If you have seen Me, you have seen the Father [or the Son or the Holy Spirit]." Logic forbids it.

And then there is the Judgment. In the Traditional Train Wreck God records our every thought and action; He catalogs with precision our good deeds and our not-so-good deeds, and then, at the end of our lives, we are judged—some to everlasting life and others to everlasting death. But before we die, we are punished for our unforgiven sins, and some suffer with many stripes (Luke 12:47). As mentioned earlier, many Christians think the wicked suffer endlessly in hell, and others think we only suffer as long as we deserve, and then experience death. Either way, God is portrayed as personally punishing His children for their bad deeds. I've heard long and descriptive sermons elaborating on the pain and suffering of those who are to writhe in hell—terrifying sermons, actually—and they made me think twice about some of the decisions I have made, but they also caused me to fear God, not the pain and suffering. I don't want to overstate this point, but the Traditional Train Wreck Theology paints a harsh picture of God. Could a loving god really torture his children, even if it is for a short time, before putting them to death?

In the Great Controversy view, God still knows our every move; He knows every thought, motive, and action, and it is also recorded somewhere in heaven's library for study. But more importantly, it is recorded in our minds. Our attitude toward others, our ability or inability to love and relate, our motives, our likes and our dislikes are all embedded in our minds. And like a computer disk, if our mind is corrupted, we won't work like we are supposed to—we will perish in God's presence. Those who are lost will experience pain and death, but it is not being dished out by our heavenly Father. God is not supernaturally keeping His children alive while He punishes them; He is not torturing us before He ends our wretched lives. Our death is the natural consequence of our attitudes, motives, and rebellion. That is what separates us from God, and the pain and suffering is the realization of what we have thrown away. When the truth of our lives is revealed to us, those of us who have chosen rebellion over faith will realize we are not fit for heaven or the companionship of holy beings. We will know for a fact that we won't be living forever in paradise with our family and friends, visiting other planets or galaxies, or walking on streets of gold. We will realize that we are not capable of living in God's majestic presence and that we have foolishly used and abused our freedom of choice. And those thoughts overwhelm us. Those lost will suffer unimaginable mental anguish. There will be weeping and gnashing of teeth. They will experience what Jesus experienced in Gethsemane and on the cross. They will suffer terribly, and they will die. They didn't need to suffer through this experience; none of us do. Jesus died to show us this truth and to warn us of the consequences so we could make an informed decision. In the Great Controversy view, God will be crying, "Why should you die? How can I let you go? How can I give you up? How often I have longed to gather you together, as a hen gathers her chicks under her wings, but you were not willing." So what else can God do? He has given us the freedom of choice.

Part 3

∘∘∘─❋─∘∘∘

Clarification

In this section ideas are discussed one at a time, in more detail, and topically: alternative endings, emergency measures, faith, the book of Romans, and more.

CHAPTER 34

Alternative Endings

Jesus was the Lamb "slain from the creation of the world" (Rev. 13:8). As soon as Satan accused God of lying about sin causing death there was no other way to prove Satan wrong—God would have to demonstrate what He meant—and no one else could do it for Him, not even the angels. Any being that isn't divine doesn't have the necessary attributes to demonstrate the truth about death and live to tell about it, and with the process being as horrific as it is, God would certainly not allow one of His creatures to experience the event unnecessarily. This death was terminal, permanent, eternal. No. God would answer the questions Himself. Not only that, the questions were about God and His policies, not the angels. Honestly, only God could answer the questions and have the truth revealed in a way that could be understood by all. Though there could have been an alternative ending for both Adam and Eve and the Jewish nation, God would still have to become mortal in order to show the truth of His statement. Even if Adam and Eve had proved themselves faithful and not succumbed to Satan's lies, one of the Trinity would still have to do what Jesus did in Gethsemane and on the cross.

This is why the scripture "and without the shedding of blood there is no forgiveness" (Heb. 9:22), is true. He died for everyone to see and to learn from, in order to remove the barrier of distrust between Himself and His creatures. He demonstrated what no one else in the universe could prove—that He did not lie, that He was trustworthy, and that He would never hurt His creatures or take away their eternal life; instead, we throw it away ourselves. Had we not seen the truth and understood the meaning of His death, we wouldn't even want forgiveness, and we wouldn't want to live within a million light years of heaven with a lying, fierce, unforgiving God; we would run the other way.

By sinning themselves, Adam and Eve muddied the water. Instead of being part of the solution, they became part of the problem. God had to simultaneously clarify to the universe what He said to Satan and work with the mess Adam and Eve created. It is the same thing in chemistry. If someone gives you a water sample from his or her well to test, say for nitrate or bacteria, but they drop it in the dirt before you analyze it, it is almost impossible to separate the soil out of the mixture in order to analyze the original constituents. Had Adam and Eve not joined in the rebellion, Christ would have soon come to Earth as a mortal and died to demonstrate the truth.

In a similar way, the Jewish nation could have had an alternative ending. Had they persistently asked God for explanations and understood why God gave the laws and why He made them offer up animal sacrifices, they could have anticipated Christ's coming, welcomed Him with open arms, listened to His teachings with open hearts, and embraced Him as their God. Christ would still need to die, but the people would not have been responsible. After concluding His teachings, Jesus would have purposely, deliberately, gone to the temple, publicly, in view of his entire realm, and died the sinner's death at the altar, in order to demonstrate that what He said in the beginning was true.

There could also be an alternative ending when Jesus comes. It doesn't have to be just a remnant being saved. The gospel could go to the world and be accepted everywhere and people be converted and globally pray and ask God to come back, meet Satan's counterfeit and have young and old alike proclaim him a fake, and see Christ come and save His people. It could happen, but the Bible suggests the reverse will be true. Few will listen to the gospel and be saved in the end.

CHAPTER 35

Healing

Healing occurs as trust in our heavenly Father grows. This healing is also part of the natural law that God has created, which can be summed up in this way: that which you most highly admire, desire, love, and imitate, you will become. Once we have confidence in His providence, His wisdom, His leadership, and His character, we are more than willing to cooperate with our Heavenly Physician. In fact, as a friend, you will probably work harder in therapy than a lowly servant; you will exercise more and take your medicine more regularly and with more dedication, zeal, and attention to detail than those who only do it because they are told to. When He gives us advice or explains what is true, we will voluntarily submit to whatever medicine He administers. He can and will heal and save all who trust Him enough to listen. God, as a physician, has never lost a patient. We may die before we are whole, but God will heal all the damage that sin has done to us (Maxwell 1992).

During Jesus's three and a half years of public ministry, most of His time was spent healing people. Many people think His healing and miracles were only done to bring people close enough to hear the traditional version of the "good news of salvation," but actually He was living out the Trust/Healing/Demonstration Model: all who trust Me can and will be healed. Sin occurs in the mind. Understood truth is the prescription. Jesus said His words are life (John 6:63). The original sin of Adam and Eve was believing that God should be feared, not trusted. Once they began to fear Him, they grew to believe He was arbitrary, exacting, and severe. If you follow the Devil's picture of God, if God were given a chance, He would roast Adam and Eve in the fires of hell. If that were really true, I'd run, too. But Christ demonstrated to the world that God is not that kind of person and that it is safe to be near Him, safe to listen to Him, and safe to trust in Him. When you trust Him and listen to Him, you will be on the road to spiritual recovery. And you are "savable" at the very moment you decide to trust Him. When God says that as soon as you trust in Him, all is well, He means it. That is really all that needs to be done. The rest, sanctification or healing, comes naturally. The healing that Jesus performed was not separate and distinct from the gospel message; it is the good news—that is the way God is. All those who place their trust in Jesus will be healed. He spent a lot of time letting people get to know Him too. Jesus's healing of people was the gospel in action. "Come to Me and be healed; trust Me and be saved." Notice there wasn't a lengthy legal description in Jesus's teachings. And notice too that healing is closely related to faith.

CHAPTER 36

Faith

If we were to boil the Bible down to one word, distill it into one idea, or precipitate just one concept which God wants most for us, it would have to be faith. Sometimes translated as "belief" and sometimes "trust," faith is what it is all about. It is the culmination of all God has ever wanted of His children. Faith is the first and the last in God's realm—the epitome, the goal, the prize. Faith is the Stanly Cup, the World Cup, the Olympic gold medal of what God desires for us to have—a real, personal, intimate relationship with Him, a relationship characterized by mutual trust.

Faith is not a faint, lighthearted assent to some set of facts or belief in a few set doctrines. Faith is a decision and a way of life that says: I can trust God. I can and I will listen to His advice. I will willingly attempt all that He suggests, and because He has shown that He doesn't lie and is willing to give His life that I might not die, I can love Him too, and with all my heart and mind and strength. Faith, then, is the end product. But that seems so easy. Why didn't God just say so in the beginning? Well, He did, but we didn't believe Him, and most still don't believe Him today. And that is why God gave all the stories and all the laws. That is why God answered Gideon's prayer with wet fleece and then dry fleece and why the high priest interceded for Israel. It is why God dreamed up the sanctuary with candles, show bread, and incense.

Developing faith is the opposite of sin. I'm not just talking about lying, cheating, and stealing sins; I'm talking about the sin that leads to all other sins—not trusting God. It's the opposite of faith. That sin is a lot worse than we give it credit. That sin sinks us deeper than we realize. And were it not because of God's great love for us, we would be doomed because of it. But God has done all of this, from Genesis to Revelation, to save us from that fate by developing our faith. Everything in the Bible has been done and written down for the expressed purpose of confirming the faith of the world's looking on and developing faith in those of us on this rebellious planet.

Though the Bible discusses faith in many places, the writer of Hebrews said it best: "Let us hold unswervingly to the hope we profess, for He who promised is faithful," and "My righteous one will live by faith" (Heb. 10:23, 38). The book of Hebrews is a terrific summary of what faith is and what the early Christians should have been able to piece together of the Old Testament's ceremonial and sacrificial services with regard to Jesus, but couldn't, and Paul explained it to them. Written just before the destruction of the temple and the sacking of Jerusalem in AD 70, the book of Hebrews and its emphasis on Christ was an important step in weaning the early Christian Jews off of the temple they adored, the feasts they relished, and the ceremonies they delighted in, in order to bond them more firmly to Christ. The message of Hebrews is: Jesus is better, so have faith.

The writer shows powerfully that Jesus is better and superior to angels, superior to their ancient heroes Moses and Abraham, and superior to all the priests. Paul shows that Christianity surpasses Judaism with a better covenant, a better sanctuary, and a better sacrifice. So have faith. All this was done to develop our faith in Him. Everything! Having shown that Christ is above all, even light years ahead of and superior to the mysterious high priest, Malchezadek, Paul comes to the climax—Hebrews 11, the faith chapter. I remember reading Hebrews 11 for the first time and being stunned by the characters that made it into the hall of fame. There are the expected greats: Moses, Enoch, and Abraham, to name a few, but the surprise comes with Rahab, Sampson, and Jephthah. These characters didn't have a sterling record, and neither do I. Maybe there is, after all, hope for me, too.

The book of Hebrews helps point out that Jesus is part of everything in the sanctuary service, and it all led into the Holy of Holies, God's presence: the show bread and manna represents Jesus, the Bread of Life; the light from the menorah represents Jesus, the Light of the World; the lamb represents Jesus, as the Lamb of God; and the high priest represents Jesus, our High Priest. In every aspect of the sanctuary service and the high priest's ministry, we see an intercessor bridging the gap between God and humanity. We see Jesus bringing us closer to God. And because of this amazing intercession we begin to appreciate, then love, our wonderful Intercessor. We are amazed that He would shed His blood for us. We are astonished that He would plead our cases before God and the onlooking universe. He did all this so you and I might stand before God as though we had never sinned. Knowing all this, we feel there is no other being in the universe who could be so wonderful, no one who could be as loving as Christ. But then we hear Jesus say several times, if you have seen Me, you have seen the Father (John 14:9). Think that through. Our Intercessor did all that He did so we could stand before God unafraid, and unashamed, but our Intercessor is also God. If there was no need for anyone to stand between us and our Intercessor-God, Jesus Christ, why then did we need an intercessor in the Old Testament? It is obvious God didn't need for us to have an intercessor; Jesus Christ is God, and no one stood between the people and Jesus. The truth is, the Israelites needed an intercessor, and getting an intercessor reduced their fear enough to be willing to approach God. They were, and most of us still are, afraid of God, and we feel more comfortable knowing we have an Intercessor.

Do you remember the situation on Mount Sinai? The people pleaded with Moses to speak to God on their behalf, "lest we die." So God allowed Moses to be their intercessor, then God gave them a high priest for an intercessor. This is how it was done by all the nations around Egypt; no one went straight to their god; everyone needed an intercessor-mediator high priest. This concept was something with which the Israelites were familiar. To them, gods were to be feared; gods required intercessors, and gods demanded blood sacrifices to appease them. The Israelites were not ready for the truth. Are we?

The sanctuary and high priest are aids to faith—they bring us to Christ, who then brings us to the Father. We thought that no one could be as loving and kind as Jesus, but now we know the truth. The Father, the Son, and the Holy Spirit are the kindest, the most loving, and the most forgiving beings in the universe. Respectfully, we do not need Jesus to intercede with the Father on our behalf—God loves us already. We pray in Jesus's name acknowledging all that Jesus did to give us this revelation, to do what no one else could do—show us the truth about our heavenly Father and Himself. Every step of the biblical process has been a step whereby we can get closer to, feel more comfortable with, and trust God more. It is not, not in any way, bringing God closer to us.

All that God has done was to develop what Hebrews 11 indicates is the end result—you and I learning to trust God in the way Adam, Eve, and the heavenly host should have trusted Him in the beginning—with all of our heart, all of our mind, and all of our strength.

To sum it up, everything God has done, everything, the whole enchilada, including the sanctuary service, the high priest's ministry, and the cross, was totally, completely, 100 percent for us, our needs, our education, and our edification, and nothing, zero, zip, nada, zero percent for God.

CHAPTER 37

Aids to Faith

I f when Jesus was here teaching the Israelites, they had been open to the truth, He wouldn't have had to teach in figures of speech. God has had to speak to us this way because we were not able or willing to hear the truth. Those methods were necessary because of our blind eyes, hard hearts, and fear. Even the disciples needed some parables explained to them now and again. At times we are just not ready to learn something new, but later, maybe next week or next year, maybe even one hundred years later, will be a more opportune time. God uses these "aids to faith" because there is no better way.

Think of all the living parables in Ezekiel. Ezekiel shaving off one-half of his beard and throwing it into the wind, cooking his food over cow dung, and lying on his left side for 390 days and then on his right side for another forty days, all to make a point that they were not willing to listen to any other way. Think of all the sanctuary imagery. Remember all the metaphors from the Psalms: "the Lord is my Shepherd I shall not want," "let me dwell in your tent forever," "let me take refuge under the shelter of your wings." And we can't forget the poetic illustrations from Solomon's Song of Songs: "Like a lily among thorns is my darling among the maidens." Where would we be without all these visual aids? The rich young ruler, the sower, the mother hen, and the lost sheep, lost coin, and lost boy, these parables are all aids to faith, but there is more. Beyond these obvious examples, God has given us: a mediator, the law, and, most notably, Jesus's death as aids to faith.

We need these aids, generally, because we think we are pretty good people and don't need a whole lot of improvement. We look around and notice we are better than Hitler, Stalin, Pol Pot, and other notorious bad guys. We notice, too, our superiority to the drunk on the corner and the drug addict begging in central park, and we think we are okay, acceptable, at least. By and large, we judge others by their actions and judge ourselves by our intentions, and don't realize we just have a different variety of cancer—false pride. We are all in trouble, we were all born estranged from God, and the Bible calls it sin. Sin is so much worse than we give it credit, and its primary symptom and most obvious diagnostic feature is denial. Oh, I'm okay; like alcoholics, we can't see our true condition. And to alert us to our near-terminal state, God has had to reach down very low, way below our bootstraps. We see some of His attempts to communicate important concepts to us and recognize only the more obvious ones. We call them parables and metaphors, but, like the Matrix, some aids to faith go deeper than the surface; they are submerged into increasingly complicated and sophisticated networks. We may or may not realize their true function. In this case, I'm talking about God's use of law and why Jesus had to die. These, too, are aids to faith. We could call these more difficult aids to faith, nested or multistaged aids, like multistage rockets, or dreams within dreams, something similar to those beautiful Russian dolls that nest two, three, four … ten dolls in one, or we can compare them to trains with multiple engines, helper engines, something that leads to something else, or something within something else. And because each rocket stage, dream, doll, or train engine has its own obvious purpose, it is easy to ignore its association and relevance to greater things—the object as a whole.

God's law is the outer and most obvious doll, dream, or engine—the first stage of the rocket. The Ten Commandments and the ceremonial laws are obviously good and have an obvious purpose—keep people happy and alive. This is a good and noble goal. It can stand on its own merits without help from the other stages.

But the law has another purpose, another nested stage to its nature. It introduces us to Jesus as our sacrificial Savior and compels people to attempt some kind of new relationship with Christ. If we are starting from scratch, as a nonbeliever, and are told we are in legal trouble with God because of all the bad things we have done, and there is only one way out, confessing our sins and asking Jesus, whom we barely know, to forgive us, to exercise a little faith, and we do it, then we have come a lot closer to Jesus and a little closer to God, the Father, even if it is only a timid relationship.

Now that we are close enough to talk to Jesus, we find there is another dreamy rabbit hole, a third nested doll or rocket stage. Jesus informs us that God is just as kind and loving as He is. This revelation does two things: it gives us confidence in what the Father is like because Jesus was the kindest and most loving person to ever breathe on this planet, but it also seems to contradict the initial reason we came to Jesus in the first place—receiving forgiveness for offending God. We came initially because we thought we were in some kind of legal trouble with the Father because of our lying, cheating, and stealing sins, and now we are perplexed. Why would God the Son have to appease God the Father? The facts don't seem to add up like they did before. There is a new dynamic tension. We have to either throw out some data to make our previous paradigm work, or we have to create a new paradigm—a new sense of reality. We have to adjust, and it is really hard to do. Now we have to search for new meanings for what we have seen and heard. We have to ask hard questions such as: why would God have to kill his Son? Does God really say love me, or I'll kill you in the end? and other questions we have raised earlier. When we ask and read on, we hear of a vast galactic battle with issues that seem to circle around God and what He is like. We hear of suspicion and intrigue, lying and betrayal, and then look again at the cross. This time when we look, we see something new—new reasons to come to God and be His friends, something we would have never seen had it not been for the law leading us to the truth: God did not lie about sin causing death. Now I see and understand God in a much clearer way. Now I come to Him out of admiration and confidence. Now I trust Him; now I have even greater faith. The law, then, in many and various nested ways, leads us to faith in the Father. The law and the cross are the greatest aids to faith in the Bible. Because we are so used to seeing the outside container only, the first doll or rocket stage, we have a hard time seeing all the clues to the inside containers, and when we do see these clues, we often see them as either anomalies, or just obscure parts of scripture, verses we don't know what to do with or can't understand. I have already mentioned several of these windows: John 15:15, John 16:26, Romans 3:24–25, Micah, Hosea, and Amos, just to name a few, but here are a few more to consider:

John 12:47: "For I did not come to judge the world but to save the world." I thought God had given all judgment to the Son. John 5:45, NKJV: "Do not think that I shall accuse you to the Father; there is one who accuses you—Moses, in whom you trust." How is it that Moses is our accuser and not God or Satan in this case? John 12:48, "There is a judge for the one who rejects me and does not accept my words; that very word which I spoke will condemn him at the last day." In the end it sounds like we condemn ourselves by how we respond to Moses's and Jesus's testimony. Colossians 1:20: "And through him to reconcile to himself all things, whether things on earth or things in heaven, by making peace through his blood, shed on the cross." How did Jesus's death make peace in heaven when the holy angels have never sinned? Did the good angels need a legal sacrifice? Did they need forgiveness for their sins? What were they looking for at the cross?

Why did Jesus have to die? To clear up the misconceptions, and to clarify what God is like so we would want to come back to Him. Jesus did not have to die to appease the Father—that denies Jesus's whole mission to reveal the Father to the world.

Do you remember the parable Jesus told to the Pharisees who were about to kill Him, the story called the tenant? He told this story to their face and in public. He told this story knowing they wouldn't catch on very fast, but they would eventually see the truth of what He said, and only then, at the end of the story, would they understand He was talking about them.

Listen to another parable: There was a landowner who planted a vineyard. He put a wall around it, dug a winepress in it and built a watchtower. Then he rented the vineyard to some farmers and moved to another place. When the harvest time approached, he sent his servants to the tenants to collect his fruit. "The tenants seized his servants; they beat one, killed another, and stoned a third. Then he sent other servants to them, more than the first time, and the tenants treated them the same way. Last of all, he sent his son to them. "They will respect my son," he said. But when the tenants saw the son, they said to each other, "This is the heir. Come, let's kill him and take his inheritance." So they took him and threw him out of the vineyard and killed him.

Therefore, when the owner of the vineyard comes, what will he do to those tenants?

"He will bring those wretches to a wretched end," they replied, "and he will rent the vineyard to other tenants, who will give him his share of the crop at harvest time."

Jesus said to them, "Have you never read in the Scriptures: 'The stone the builders rejected has become the cornerstone; the Lord has done this, and it is marvelous in our eyes'? Therefore I tell you that the kingdom of God will be taken away from you and given to a people who will produce its fruit. Anyone who falls on this stone will be broken to pieces; anyone on whom it falls will be crushed."

When the chief priests and the Pharisees heard Jesus's parables, they knew he was talking about them. They looked for a way to arrest him, but they were afraid of the crowd because the people held that he was a prophet. (Matt. 21:31–46)

The Pharisees were not willing or able to accept Jesus or His message at that time. They struggled with this paradox: Jesus's life and teachings didn't seem to mesh with their understanding of the Messiah. They couldn't see the two as equal. Jesus gave them reason after reason for believing in Him, including this and many other parables.

Later, after Jesus's death and resurrection, many of the Pharisees and rulers reconsidered Jesus's aids to faith, changed their minds, and became ardent followers. They just were not ready to hear what He had to say at the time.

In a similar fashion, many people's understanding of God's use of law is still pending. The law that is our schoolmaster to bring us to Christ is all law; it is both the ceremonial and the moral law. The legal aspects of scripture were all meant to bring us to God, but we are not to stay there; we are to press on to an ever closer relationship with our friendly God. The hard part in Galatians is this: after we come to Christ there is no more need for the schoolmaster; there is no more need to bring up the condemning aspects of law. Galatians 3 is still an enigma within the Christian Community, but doesn't need to be. Genuine faith is all God has ever required.

CHAPTER 38

————∘∘∘❦❦❦∘∘∘————

God's Use of Law

G od's use of law has always been the issue. It was debated in heaven with Lucifer. It was questioned in the garden of Eden with Adam and Eve. It was added to at Mount Sinai with the giving of the Ten Commandments and expanded when God gave the statutes and rules for the sanctuary service. God added health laws and laws for their government, too. God's laws became an issue with the early Christian church with circumcision, and they are misunderstood even today.

This begs the question, why did God give all these laws? What was His purpose? Are they still relevant? Should we be doing or not doing something that these laws point out? And, what happens if we don't follow some of them?

Galatians chapter 3 makes a bold statement: What is the purpose of the law? It was added. Generally we try to ferret out which law was added, but it was all law. Health, civil, dietary, ceremonial, and even the Ten Commandments have been added. In the beginning, before the rebellion, no one needed to be reminded to love; but as we have degraded, God has had to add and add and add new laws to help us out.

Understanding why God gave these laws is important even if we decide they are not to be kept; we may still find some principles that are worth remembering.

God gave civil laws that were important for organizing Israel. They camped in organized patterns, marched in organized precision, and operated an organized judicial system. Are these laws binding on Christians around the world today? No. But are they instructive? Yes. Having an organized society, government, military, and judicial system is very important. What are the consequences for not being organized? Chaos. The disaster grows as the population increases. Though not binding, seeing how God organized Israel could be very helpful.

What about the sanitary health laws, are they binding? Leviticus 13–15, for example, has laws for leprosy, boils, and burns, terrible diseases that can be easily spread.

If a person showed signs of infection, God had instructed the priests to first determine if the disease was spreading or contagious. They would isolate the patient for seven days. If the boil faded in color or shrank in size, he or she would be declared "clean." If not, they would be put out of the camp. If the disease or boil were to go away the person would send word to the priest. The priest would meet the person at the edge of the city and check the infection. If the infection was gone, he could shave off all the hair on his body, wash his clothes, bathe, and then go into town, but he could not go to his dwelling for seven more days. At the end of seven days, he was to repeat the shaving of his body, including eyebrows, wash his clothes, and bathe again; then life could go on as normal.

Along with all the cleaning, the person was to make an offering. As soon as he was allowed to come back into the camp, two birds were used in a special ceremony. Then, on the eighth day a male lamb was to be sacrificed if the person could afford one.

Are these laws binding upon Christians today? No. Are they instructive? Yes. Today we call leprosy Hansen's disease, and in the house we have mold and dry rot. But the remedies we use today are the same ones God gave Israel. They were thousands of years ahead of the heathen people around them. What are the consequences of living in filth and human waste, and of drinking polluted water? Pandemics, cholera, plague, and more. During the fourteenth century the bubonic plague killed twenty-four million people, over one third of the European population. If they had practiced the laws in Leviticus, the death toll could have been much lower. The health laws, though not binding today, are followed because the consequences for not following them are severe.

What about the dietary laws God gave? Are they still to be followed? Usually when dietary restrictions are raised, people are thinking of Leviticus 11, the clean and unclean foods, and the discussion spirals down to: can we eat bacon? But God started the dietary discussion in Eden when He specified that Adam and Eve were to eat plants having seeds (Gen. 1:29). That would mean fruits, grains, and nuts. After God withheld the Tree of Life, He allowed vegetables—you have to kill the plant normally to eat carrots, beets, and potatoes. Though not everyone followed the meal plan, after the flood some animals were allowed, possibly because the flood ruined the planet, and there wasn't much else to eat. It takes years for an almond tree or pecan tree to produce nuts. So God allowed clean animals to be eaten. After being released from Egypt and again finding little to eat in the desert, God gave Israel manna. I don't know how long He would have supplied them with those sweet morsels, but manna was God's food of choice for Israel and not the other alternatives. So that brings us back to Leviticus 11. God gave Israel a long list of what to eat and what not to eat, calling some clean and others unclean.

Are these laws still binding on Christians today? Are those critters still "unclean"? There is still some debate about this. The book of Acts makes it crystal clear that Gentiles are not to be considered unclean. In a trance Peter saw a large tablecloth rising to heaven with all kinds of unclean animals in it and heard God tell him, "Rise, Peter, kill and eat." (Acts 11) And just minutes later a Gentile came to Peter's house to hear the gospel. Peter went with the man knowing, "that no man should be considered common or unclean." But did this vision of Peter's have a double meaning? Was God declaring all meat "clean"? Many Christians think so. If God was declaring all animals clean, did this declaration make the food any healthier? Did He perform a miracle and change the cellular structure of sharks and eels? Should we eat tarantulas because there are no laws against it? Probably not. We don't go and do everything we want just because there isn't a law against it, do we? Do we need to be told everything? For example, He didn't declare eating animals already dead—road kill—unclean and then send down a special curse if anyone ate it or if they ate an eagle or snake. Eating these animals had serious liabilities. They may have died of mad cow disease or worse!

God didn't give these rules and then add punishments for disobeying them, and then with the Christian dispensation decide to remove the punishments. He was alerting us to factors that were beyond our comprehension at the time. They didn't know about vitamins, minerals, fiber, calories, protein, and carbohydrates, and they didn't know about bacteria and viruses, and that refrigeration retards their growth. They didn't know about bleach, Pine-Sol, plastic gloves or any of the things scientists have taught us. We have learned a lot since Moses wrote down Leviticus. Today we can make more informed choices. We don't need a list of good and bad foods. Today if God were to make a list it may include: cigarettes, marijuana, pop, chips, and too much pie and ice cream. He might even add a section on exercise, and for me a section on too much exercise.

Like the other laws God gave, if you don't abide by the "rules," what are the results? You just reap the natural consequences.

God gave Israel a ton of laws for the two-roomed sanctuary, and more laws for the priests and high priests. He gave laws for the altar, candlesticks, incense, and the Ark. He also commanded they attend feasts. Seven festivals were scattered across the Hebrew calendar. Each feast was instructive: the Passover commemorated the tenth plague on Egypt and how they were spared. The Feast of Unleavened Bread was to remind them that with haste they left the land of Egypt. First Fruits was the only feast held on Sunday; it commemorated the first of the barley harvest, but also prefigured Jesus's resurrection. Pentecost occurred fifty days later, and it celebrated the end of the harvest, prefiguring the outpouring of the Holy Spirit. The Feast of Trumpets announced Yom Kippur, the Day of Atonement, which was solemn, all the people reflecting on their sins of the past and asking for forgiveness. It celebrated the wiping away of sins, prefiguring the Judgment. And last, after the weary year, the Feast of Booths was a time of rest, and someday we too will all rest in heaven, and eventually back on the Earth made new.

Are these feasts and ceremonies mandatory? Are we still obligated to keep these laws? No. These rituals were to help bring the Israelites to Christ and help identify Him when He came. Though this did not work for many, there is much we can learn from these laws and God's way of communicating to us.

So far I don't think I've said anything controversial, as most everyone agrees that many of the rules found in the Old Testament were just for Israel, and a wise person (or county) can learn a lot from what God gave Israel. But what about the Ten Commandments? Are they the same as the other laws, or are they on a higher plane? Are they more than just good suggestions? Are they mandatory?

The Bible talks a lot about law. It is in every crack and crevice. Have you ever wondered why? Well, why do you tell your children not to put knives into wall sockets, or look both ways before crossing the street, or don't drink and drive? Is it because you want to limit their freedom or to preserve their freedom? Is it possible to look at the Ten Commandments like we did the other laws, as God just pointing out things to watch out for? Think about your future life for a moment. Would you like to live forever with people who lie to your face, want to cheat you out of your diamond-studded crown, and steal your fruity breakfast from the Tree of Life? And would you like to live with people who have no love or respect for your heavenly Father, people who really don't want to spend any time getting to know Him? Me either. The Ten Commandments are basic High School 101—how to live a good life and let others live too. Like the other laws God has given, even if they were repealed, changed from "clean" to "unclean," and He took them off the wall, would you want to get rid of them?

But are they mandatory? I hope so. I don't want to live forever in a world like this one. But the real question is not, should we love God and each other? It's cleverly hidden: what will happen if I don't keep the Commandments? Notice, we are just as free to observe or not observe these laws as we are with the dietary and civil laws. Just look around. People do terrible things all the time. But because God respects our freedom of choice, He does not step in. But there are consequences.

Based upon how God allows the natural consequences to prevail with His other laws, and considering Jesus's death, I think it is obvious what God will do to those who don't want to love: He'll let them go and give them up to the consequences. However, the consequences of not loving each other and God are much more critical than deciding to forgo a high cholesterol lunch, but both come with natural consequences.

Everything in life has consequences. We can't avoid it. But if we think before we act, we can be on the receiving end of the best consequences.

CHAPTER 39

Emergency Measures

Some people have suggested that the Demonstration Model makes God into a big marshmallow, a softy on sin. They ask: what about all the tough guy stories in the Bible? What about all the fire and brimstone and curses and wrath? A lot of stories, especially in the Old Testament, seem harsh and appear to support Satan's claims, that is, if we don't look closely from a Great Controversy perspective. Why did God speak and act so harshly when He had been accused of being just that way by Satan? Well, God certainly took some great risks with the potential to be misunderstood, but He evidently felt the reward was worth the hazards. God has suffered many things in this war. He has even risked His reputation to save as many as He could—even if His actions might make Him look harsh at the moment. The list of stories that fall into this "risky" category is long, and I hate to keep repeating them, but they are fundamental:

- God kicks Adam and Eve out of the Garden after their first mistake.
- God floods the world to save eight.
- God turns Lot's wife into salt.
- God thunders on Mount Sinai.
- God kills the Egyptians' firstborn male children.

- God helps the Israelites wipe out the nations in Canaan.
- God commands the stoning of the Sabbath-breaker.
- God destroys Korah, Dathan, Abiram, and their friends and family.
- God helps Gideon's 300 men kill over 120,000 Midianites.
- God helps Samson destroy a thousand Philistines with a jawbone.
- God helps David kill Goliath.
- God uses an angel to kill 185,000 Assyrians.
- God helps Elijah when he calls down fire on Mount Carmel, and kills 450 false prophets.
- God helps Elisha kill forty children with she-bears.
- God orders the Israelites to divorce all of their heathen wives.

And on and on.

These stories, instead of making God look bad, actually do the opposite. If you consider the gigantic personal risk involved for God to do what He did, to risk appearing just as Satan accused Him of being, so He could save a few more of us on this rebellious planet, you will see these stories and God in a different light. God was willing to look like a tyrant at times if it might compel any of us rebels to get off the train tracks long enough to look up and listen. They are emergency measures.

Like most people, I prize my reputation, and as a Christian I especially guard it lest I become a blight on my family, the church, and on God. But God risked it all—including His reputation. He humbled Himself and became a man, humbled Himself more and became a servant, and continued to humble Himself by dying to demonstrate the consequences of sin.

But some of the hardest and most humiliating times for God were when He did things that made it look like Satan was right, times when He had to look unforgiving and severe to make some important statement or to get our attention. It was hard for God to discipline Israel and look harsh to the onlooking universe; it was hard for God to help Israel kill the Egyptians, Assyrians, Korah, Dathan, and Abiram, and look severe in the eyes of the worlds looking on; it was hard for God to kill those forty rebellious, disrespectful youth (they are His children, too); it was hard for God to command the Israelites to divorce their mates, and it is really hard, especially when you have the power to heal cancer, brain tumors, blindness, and every other type of disease, but won't, even when your children pray, because you have to show the awful effects of sin. In doing so, millions of God's children see Him as either impotent or uncaring.

You, too, I'm sure, want to protect your reputation. If you were accused of stealing from work, wouldn't you do everything in your power to be seen as upright? But God cared more about us than protecting His already tainted and tarnished reputation because He loves His children so. We see that He did it just to save a few more people. In reality, He loves you and me more than He loves Himself or His short-term reputation.

If sin were merely breaking God's rules, these emergency measures would appear vengeful, severe, and hypocritical. But what if sin is not just something that needs forgiveness from time to time, but something that causes real damage in people. What if it is something that needs real healing and for which the natural consequence is a forever death. And if millions of worlds are looking down at this planet to see what God is really like under pressure, then what we are seeing is God doing everything He can, in every way He can, meeting people where they are, leading them only as fast as they can follow, and trying to rescue each of us from eternal death. He is trying to keep us from making that final, fatal mistake of rejecting Him.

When your children run into a busy street or onto train tracks, you don't just whisper, "Oh, children, don't go out there today." You scream at the top of your lungs all kinds of threats and promises to get their attention; you jump up and down; you get red in the face; you do everything within your power to get them to turn back before it is too late.

Assuming it is our rejection of God and not His anger for our disobedience that causes death, let's examine a few of the above-mentioned stories from a Great Controversy perspective. When God kicked Adam and Eve out of the Garden, did He do that because they merely disobeyed and needed punishing? No. He did it because if He hadn't, they wouldn't have learned the lessons they needed to learn. Out in the field, they would see the results of sin: death in flowers and plants, disease, sickness, pain, sorrow, and the Garden would still be there for comparison. These are the results of rejecting God. It is sin that causes death, not God, but they wouldn't have learned that lesson in the perfect garden of Eden. God had to do something drastic to meet the emergency. On the other hand, how would it look if it really were God kicking His children out of the house for their first mistake? Do you severely punish your children for their first failure? The offense could not have been just disobedience, but a decision that God couldn't be trusted. A decision that if not reversed, would be fatal.

On Mount Sinai, God shook and thundered. Why didn't He speak softly like He did on the Mount of Olives? Answer: the Israelites had been slaves of the Egyptians for more than four hundred years. As if they had amnesia, they forgot about God. They became spiritually debased, almost barbaric in their beliefs and actions. They had become so accustomed to the heathen religions around them that the only thing that would impress them was raw power. So, God showed them a little of His power in the ten plagues, and more power at Mount Sinai with lightning, thunder, and earthquakes, but evidently it wasn't enough to develop respect for Him, because they were worshiping idols again in forty days. God had to make an impression because of the type of people with which He was dealing. God loves every one of us, including the Israelites that left Egypt, so He met them where they were, not wanting any of them to suffer the second death. How do you think they would have responded to a gentle "Blessed are the meek; blessed are the poor" sermon?

This story is encouraging to me. If I'm straying and in need of discipline, some Sinai language or a little earthquake and fire, God will give me what I need. It is actually hard to be lost. God puts roadblocks in our way, trials in our path, people in our lives, and the Holy Spirit in our hearts to help lead us to Him, and home.

It also seems strange that our loving God would ever help people kill other people, especially when He has given a commandment that says do not murder. Even though God said He would clear the way for the Israelites to enter Canaan using hornets, He allowed them to kill the inhabitants in their own way. He even helped because He wanted to keep in touch with His people. Just as in the time of the flood, if God didn't help clean out the unbelieving people around the Israelites, He would have lost His people completely, and the demonstration would have ground to a halt. God can and will resurrect all those who are able to be saved. There may have been many people killed throughout history who were good who will rise in the first resurrection. The flood, the killing of the Canaanites, the killing of the Assyrians, and the other killing stories are emergency measures used to inspire confidence in His ability to lead, protect, and inspire respect in His people.

Along the same lines, why did God command the Israelites to divorce their heathen wives (Ezra 10)? After all, doesn't God hate divorce (Mal. 2:16)? Earlier in history, the Israelites were overcome by the heathen nations around them and were seduced by the beautiful women from the surrounding nations into worshiping heathen Gods. They wanted to be good, but they fell short through intermarrying. Even Solomon, the wisest man in history, was not able to resist these heathen temptresses, and made a shipwreck of his life and the nation. After Israel's apostasy, God allowed the Israelites to languish in Babylonian captivity to discipline them. And, after He brought them out of captivity, they started intermarrying again with heathen people. What should God have done? Should He have ignored the problem hoping it would go away? Would they have more luck than Solomon this time? Should He have told the Israelites, "Go, and give the pagan women Bible studies; take all the time you need; see if you can win a few"? Like before, if God were to leave His people alone and let them continue down those tracks, He would have lost them again to idolatry. What else could God do in this difficult situation but give the command: divorce your heathen wives, but do it in a proper way. God has resorted to emergency measures time and time again, but these are not God's preferred methods for dealing with His children. When your children are running out onto train tracks, you use emergency measures. But if your next-door neighbor is watching and didn't fully understand the situation, he might think you were exacting and severe. God ran a gigantic risk of being misunderstood, but what else could a loving Father do?

CHAPTER 40

Is It Legal?

Is salvation a legal arrangement? Yes and no. The biblical narrative and salvation can be explained both ways, but it depends on whose perspective you are interested in. In the beginning of the war, Satan could only see sin and salvation as a legal arrangement and thought he was being cheated. The angels looking on were confused and unsure about the issues; thus salvation probably appeared to be a legal arrangement to them as well, at least until they witnessed Gethsemane and the cross. Humans, too, understand in legal terms until we are developmentally mature enough to do otherwise. As small children, we only know that "might is right." Later we mature and understand concepts of right and wrong, black and white, obey and disobey; we understand the concepts of law and look at the Bible and God's offer as a legal transaction, merely. However, for most of us, maturity continues, and we learn to conceptualize natural consequences and gray areas. We do what is right, because it is right, not just because there are laws that say so. As mature Christians, we can see sin and salvation in nonlegal terms. God, our Creator, knowing what we can and cannot comprehend, has explained sin and salvation in terms we can recognize and appreciate; He has instructed us in ways appropriate for our maturity. To explain law, sin, and our calamitous predicament to the vast majority of us, it was best to explain it first in legal terms, because we all go through that developmental stage, and it is a better motivator for people who are afraid of God to begin with. This was the most effective way God could bring us to Christ, and keep us there, at least until He could explain salvation in more precise terms. But the truth is: God does not see sin in legal terms, and that is why we see the two concepts blended in scripture.

God sees sin like a physician sees a dying patient. Whether it is pancreatic cancer or a head-on collision with a bus, what He sees are His children in pain and about to die without His help. Sin is not a legal problem with God; it is a real problem. And if we are not won back to trust Him, we die.

Without God in our lives, (and it isn't always obvious who does and who doesn't because the Holy Spirit works with all of His human family), we act like we are on a lifeboat with not enough room for everyone aboard. And to preserve ourselves, we minimize the others. We are not very creative as children and literally push others off the boat, but as adults we are more sophisticated and use money, position, IQ, pedigree, sarcasm, and letters after our name to do the shoving for us.

So we have two explanations of the plan of salvation in the Bible. What do we do with them both? Do we get rid of one in preference of the other? I believe if we look at God's previous methods of teaching and evangelism, we should see where the student is first. Some may need the training wheels that come with the legal model. They may be terrified of God and need an intercessor; they can transition later. But others, especially those who are not afraid of God to begin with, should learn the demonstration model right away.

This is nothing more than applying Galatians chapter 3. Paul said that the law was added. That includes the entire legal system with its associated legal language of the atonement. But after coming to Christ, now as friends (John 15:15), there is no more need for the schoolmaster, no more need to explain the plan of salvation in legal terms. The Great Controversy-Demonstration model should, however, become the predominant teaching. People can handle the concepts; I know twelve-year-olds who understand it. We don't give people enough credit. We need to allow people to grow up spiritually. Jesus started telling the people of His day the bigger picture by healing them. They didn't know it was the gospel. They were just amazed at His power to heal and cast out demons, and by healing them, Jesus surely demonstrated His love and concern. But like many things God does, those healings had additional significance. Healing is the best way to illustrate the plan of salvation from God's perspective. Come to Me and be healed; trust Me and be whole! If salvation was a legal transaction merely, and Christ wanted to illustrate the legal plan of salvation in the best way possible, then shouldn't He have taken on the role of a trial lawyer? Israel had lawyers in the first century. What if Jesus had come to the world as a lawyer or judge, instead of a healer? How would that have changed history?

CHAPTER 41

―∘∘⊶⧓⊷∘∘―

Know

Many words in the Bible are powerful; they have more meaning than what first meets the eye, such as: faith, wrath, death, and know. The word *know* does not mean that I have heard of something new, and now *know* it, or you and I have accumulated some additional facts, and now *know* more, but is used to indicate there is a special, positive, intimate relationship between the two parties: they trust each other; they are lovers, or they are close personal friends. In Genesis it says that Adam *knew* Eve, and Eve gave birth to a son (Gen. 4:1). Jesus said, "If you really *knew* me, you would *know* my Father as well" (John 14:7). This personal knowing, trusting relationship is what God has always wanted, and He says in John 17, when this is achieved, you have eternal life.

> Father, the time has come. Glorify Your Son, that Your Son may glorify You. For You granted Him authority over all people that He might give eternal life to all those You have given Him. Now *this is eternal life: that they may know You, the only true God and Jesus Christ, whom You have sent.* I have brought You glory on earth by *completing the work You gave Me to do.* (John 17:1–4)

In an opposite manner, those who don't really "know" the Lord will not be saved. Consider this parable of Jesus:

> Then Jesus went through the towns and villages, teaching as he made his way to Jerusalem. Someone asked him, "Lord, are only a few people going to be saved?" He said to them, "Make every effort to enter through the narrow door, because many, I tell you, many will try to enter and will not be able to. Once the owner of the house gets up and closes the door, you will stand outside knocking and pleading, 'Sir, open the door for us.' But he will answer, 'I don't *know* you or where you come from.' Then you will say, 'We ate and drank with you, and you taught in our streets.' But he will reply, 'I don't *know* you or where you come from. Away from Me all you evil doers.'" (Luke 13:22–27)

God knows every one of us; He even knows how many hairs we have on our heads. How is it, then, that He could say, "I don't *know* you?" Because, He's talking about knowing us in a personal, meaningful, deep spiritual, and friendly way, not some superficial or formal, mechanical relationship. The Pharisees thought they could get by on just a formal legal relationship, too, and Jesus commented on that:

> You search the Scriptures, for in them you think you have eternal life; and these are they which testify of Me. (John 5:39, NKJV)

In these verses, where does Jesus ever bring up believing in His ability to vicariously, legally, die and forgive them of their sins? He just said, *eternal life is knowing God.* All of His teachings reflect this notion. Knowing God is everything. He is the best there is in music, poetry, chemistry, physics, kindness, compassion, forgiveness, pity, love—God has no equal, and wants to share all of these with you and me.

CHAPTER 42

A New Perspective on Romans

any of you have studied the Bible for years, and most likely the same way I did—here a little and there a little. But after growing tired of just linking verses together I decided to read through the Bible chronologically, and I did it several times a year for several years. Later, I was able to listen to the Bible book by book during long car trips and while commuting to work. I found the Bible was immensely more than twenty or thirty or even fifty distinct doctrines. It was really just one story with hundreds of small jewels of truth coalescing into a unified whole—a revelation of what God is like, and demonstrated under many and various circumstances. I found I was really missing out by making my here a little and there a little—too little—and when I enlarged the context to include a massive war in heaven wherein God was accused of being a certain way and lying about sin, well, I felt like I knew God in a better, more personal way. It was like having a second conversion. I wanted to be like Moses, Abraham, Job, and Elijah, one of God's true friends. After trying to explain this to several people, I found that the way a person reads the book of Romans is key. We have read it piece by piece for so long, linking short little verses together just to prove some doctrinal point, that we have a hard time seeing the book in a larger context. Instead, give Romans another chance by reading it as one continuous letter. Read it in its own context, and don't quit until you get to the end—read the letter as a whole.

Like all of scripture, you don't know the real story unless you know the background. The background for the entire Bible is a universe-wide war. But to add to this, part of the context of all of Paul's writings is the contrast between Paul's former beliefs as a zealous Pharisee and his beliefs and attitudes after his miraculous conversion.

Paul's Story

I watched a squabble in the street and recognized the Christian, Stephen, in the middle of it. I listened intently. I heard an amazing summary of the history of my people. His speech was true, clear, precise, and it laid the blame for Jesus's death squarely on me and my people.

> You stiff-necked people, with uncircumcised hearts and ears! You are just like your fathers: You always resist the Holy Spirit! Was there ever a prophet your fathers did not persecute? They even killed those who predicted the coming of the Righteous One. And now you have betrayed and murdered him—you who have received the law that was put into effect through angels but have not obeyed it. (Acts 7:51–53)

Stephen spoke boldly and without fear, showing we were the ones who broke the law—not Jesus. The Jews looking on were enraged at the accusation and rushed in to kill him. Stephen's face lit up like a lantern, his resolve was hard as a rock. He proclaimed he could see Jesus in heaven standing on God's right side (which only made matters worse), and they mauled him. At the end Stephen cried out, "Father, forgive them; don't hold this sin against them." But I consented to the lynching; I held the coats of those who stoned Stephen in my arms and at my feet.

How could this deluded heretic know the scriptures so well? How could someone pray for their slayer while being stoned? And why did it appear as though his face was glowing like Moses's?

With these memories in mind and my conscience aroused, I continued to fight for the "faith," defend the church, and stamp out this "heresy" wherever I could find it. I'd do anything to quell my conscience. I was shameless, heartless, and ruthless in my persecution of the Christians, throwing them in jail and chasing them from town to town. I was living out my unspoken belief that God is vengeful and had no problem persecuting those who didn't believe the "truth." Exacting, I made them pay for the smallest insubordination. Unforgiving and severe, I had no mercy on those teaching this "heresy" as I threw them into prison or worse.

Months later, as part of a raiding party, I rode my horse, anxiously, with grit in my teeth and wind in my hair, galloping, my companions behind me straining to keep up, a summons in my pouch, and a sword stashed in my sheath. I was going to Damascus to kill Christians.

While riding, what looked like lightning and what sounded like thunder struck. We were all thrown to the ground. I couldn't see. I could barely hear. Like a boxer punched in the nose before the beginning bell, I was stunned—my eyes burning, tiny fires blazing each time I blinked. I found myself lying on my back, spitting dirt, and wondering why I couldn't see. Then I heard God's voice thunder, "Saul, Saul, why are you persecuting me?" "Who are you, Lord?" I replied. "I am Jesus," came the voice (Acts 9:4). For several seconds, minutes maybe, I lay there summing up the situation. I realized I was in trouble. I had been persecuting the followers of Jesus. I thought I had seconds to live. If I knew God, and I thought I did, God's fiery wrath would kill me quickly.

Would the Earth open up like it did for Korah? Would it be bears or a plague? I didn't know which, but I knew it was coming. After all, that is exactly what I would do if I were in God's shoes. But nothing happened.

God said:

"Now get up and go into the city, and you will be told what you must do."

The men traveling with Saul stood there speechless; they heard the sound but did not see anyone. Saul got up from the ground, but when he opened his eyes he could see nothing. So they led him by the hand into Damascus. For three days he was blind, and did not eat or drink anything. (Acts 9:6–9)

What do you think Saul was thinking about for three days? He had 20-20 vision the day before, and now he's blind, doomed to be led around by the hand and begging for his breakfast. He had been killing Christians. He thought God would kill him after a little revenge and torture. For three days I'm sure he prayed and recited in his mind all of the Bible memory texts he knew. Being a disciple of Gamalial, he may have had most of the Old Testament memorized. He may have remembered some of the blessings and cursings from Deuteronomy 28:

If you do not obey the Lord your God and do not carefully follow all his commands and decrees I am giving you today, all these curses will come upon you and overtake you: You will be cursed in the city and cursed in the country. Your basket and your kneading trough will be cursed. The fruit of your womb will be cursed, and the crops of your land, and the calves of your herds and the lambs of your flocks. You will be cursed when you come in and cursed when you go out. Your carcasses will be food for all the birds of the air and the beasts of the earth, and there will be no one to frighten them away. The Lord will afflict you with the boils of Egypt and with tumors, festering sores and the itch, from which you cannot be cured.

And it ends:

> The Lord will afflict you with madness, *blindness,* and
> confusion of mind. At midday you will grope about like
> a blind man in the dark. You will be unsuccessful in
> everything you do; day after day you will be oppressed
> and robbed, with no one to rescue you. (Deut. 28:15–29)

Paul may have been thinking of all the vengeance passages in the
Bible, too. There are over thirty places where God promises vengeance
on His enemies, and 166 times the Old Testament speaks of wrath. Saul
knew that he was now considered one of God's enemies.

- Rejoice, O nations, with his people, for he will avenge the blood
  of his servants; he will take *vengeance* on his enemies and make
  atonement for his land and people. (Deut. 32:43)
- When I sharpen my flashing sword and my hand grasps it in
  judgment, I will take *vengeance* on my *adversaries and repay those
  who hate me.* (Deut. 32:41)

That is a lot of cursing and vengeance and wrath! Saul was scared
out of his skin. I would be too. Have you ever been so afraid that you
couldn't swallow? Have you ever seen a car or truck coming your way at
seventy miles per hour and thought it is all over? Have you ever raced a
train through a railroad crossing, and cut it way too close? Usually it is
quick, but for Paul, he had to sit and think about it, for three long days.

> Then Ananias went to the house and entered it. Placing
> his hands on Saul, he said, "Brother Saul, the Lord—
> Jesus, who appeared to you on the road as you were
> coming here—has sent me so that you may see again and
> be filled with the Holy Spirit." Immediately, something
> like scales fell from Saul's eyes, and he could see again.
> (Acts 9:17–18)

Can you imagine the excitement Paul must have felt? After three days of living in terror and dread of the future, Paul was ecstatic; God didn't leave him blind. God hadn't struck him down. He didn't intimidate Saul any further. He just sent him away and had him think about it.

It may have taken Paul a while, but he found out the truth about God's supposed harshness—that it is discipline. Paul was going up the train tracks and into the tunnel when God floored him on the road to Damascus. God gave Saul three days to think and fear before showing him the gracious truth: God disciplines those He loves, and His wrath is the horrendous natural consequences of Him finally letting you go, giving you up after a long, hard battle and not something He does out of anger.

It might have taken Paul a few years to figure it all out. He didn't really get into the ministry "full-throttle" for about thirteen or fourteen more years. He spent a few years in Arabia and a few years in Tarsus. He spent some time in Jerusalem, Syria, and Cilicia, all before Barnabas retrieved him from Tarsus and brought him to Antioch (Acts 11:25). But when Paul got going, he was as zealous for the Lord as he ever was, but this time with a different picture of God.

Paul's first missionary journey was the shortest in time and distance of the three. Paul, Barnabus, and Mark sailed to Cyprus and then north to present-day Turkey, where Mark left to go back home to Jerusalem. Paul and Barnabus continued to Iconium, Lystra, and Derbe before backtracking to Antioch in Seleucia. The tour took about two years.

On Paul's second missionary journey, he visited Corinth. Corinth had plenty of problems, serious problems, and that is a story in itself, but when things smoothed out, he had time to write to Rome and Galatia. Now, considering Paul's background, what topics do you think he wanted to inspire in the believers of Rome and Galatia? He was writing to Gentiles and fellow Jews with the same history and picture of God that he used to have. Two topics Paul wanted to stress led to a third:

1. What Saul had previously thought were expressions of God's "righteous" anger, were actually emergency measures designed

to keep His children from self-destruction. Like the lightning that blinded him on the road to Damascus, Paul discovered that God disciplines those He loves.

2. Closely related to this, Saul found that God's wrath is God finally letting His children go—to reap the tragic natural consequences of their choices. These two new concepts changed Saul's picture of God and led to:

3. Now, Paul had new reasons to obey God: love, respect, and trust. His old obedience was centered on gaining rewards and escaping punishments—on law—but now Paul had a new and better reason to obey—faith. He found that the law was intended to bring us to Christ, so we could be set right by faith.

Observe how Paul addresses all of these concepts in the first chapter of Romans and then discusses directly why Jesus died in chapter three:

> Paul, a servant of Christ Jesus, called to be an apostle and set apart for the *gospel of God*—the *gospel* he promised beforehand through his prophets in the Holy Scriptures *regarding His Son*. ... to call people from among all the Gentiles to the *obedience that comes from faith*. ... For I am not ashamed of the *gospel of Christ*, for it is the power of God to salvation for everyone who believes, for the Jew first and also for the Greek. For in it the *righteousness of God* is revealed from faith to faith; as it is written, *"The just shall live by faith."*

> For the *wrath of God is revealed* from heaven against all ungodliness and unrighteousness of men, who suppress the truth in unrighteousness, because what may be known of God is manifest in them, for God has shown it to them. ... Therefore *God also gave them up* to uncleanness, in the lusts of their hearts, to dishonor their bodies among themselves, who *exchanged the truth of God for the lie*, and worshiped and served the creature rather than the Creator, who is blessed forever. Amen.

For this reason *God gave them up* to vile passions. For even their women exchanged the natural use for what is against nature. Likewise also the men, leaving the natural use of the woman, burned in their lust for one another, men with men committing what is shameful, and receiving in themselves the penalty of their error which was due. And even as they did not like to retain God in their knowledge, *God gave them over* to a debased mind. (Rom. 1:1–28, NKJV)

Whom God set forth *as* a propitiation by His blood, through faith, *to demonstrate His righteousness*, because in His forbearance God had passed over the sins that were previously committed, to **demonstrate** at the present time *His righteousness*, that He might be **just** and the justifier of the one who has faith in Jesus. (Rom. 3: 25–26, NJKV)

Paul continues these themes throughout the next sixteen chapters, weaving in stories of Abraham and others in order to bring the point home.

After his Damascus Road experience, outwardly, had Paul changed much? Did he still go to the same church? Did he still call God by the same name and in the same way? Did he still keep Sabbath? Did Paul still eat the same foods, did he still pay a tithe, believe in the sanctuary system, and believe in the same scriptures? Was he still zealous for God, even more so? It is interesting that Saul was on Satan's side before his conversion and on the Lord's side after being floored on the road to Damascus, yet you would have to look close to know there was a difference, because he was still sitting in the same pew and reading the same books. There was a difference, but it wasn't the normal church doctrines that changed. What did change? His picture of God changed. Now he had a new understanding of why Jesus had to die. Now, he obeyed out of love, respect, and faith.

Because of Paul's new understanding of God, he was even more in love with God. To him, the good news was: God was *not* like what he had been taught. Now, Paul could brag like Jeremiah.

> This is what the Lord says: "Let not the wise man boast of his wisdom or the strong man boast of his strength or the rich man boast of his riches, but let him who boasts boast about this: that he understands and knows me, that I am the Lord, who exercises kindness, justice and righteousness on earth, for in these I delight," declares the Lord. (Jer. 9:23–24)

CHAPTER 43

Fiery Furnace

What characteristics do all evil people seem to have in common? What marks their depravity? Some have amiable traits of character such as charm or charisma. Some are good looking and have a commanding presence. They may even love their friends; but when push comes to shove, they prefer to destroy. They take the low road of force, fear, and intimidation. Take Hitler for example. After rising to power, claiming that his one desire was to reestablish Germany's lofty world status and dignity, he sunk to using torture, murder, chemical weapons, and psychological warfare to get what he wanted. It's a good thing they never built the "bomb"!

One ancient analog to Hitler may have been King Nebuchadnezzar of Babylon. They both conquered nations and ruled with an iron fist, but Nebuchadnezzar killed dissenters with a blast furnace instead of nerve gas and tiger tanks. If he was disobeyed it was off to the flames, not the showers.

Early in Nebuchadnezzar's career, God gave him a vision of the future (Dan 2). In a dream he saw a gigantic metallic statue with a gold head, silver chest and arms, a bronze waist, iron legs, and iron and clay feet and toes. Each metal represented a kingdom, and each successive kingdom was inferior to the former. The gold head represented Nebuchadnezzar and Babylon, the silver chest and arms represented the

Meads and Persians, the bronze belly and thighs—Greece, the iron legs—Rome, and the iron and clay feet and toes—Europe, the fallen Roman Empire. Daniel interpreted the dream for Nebuchadnezzar who bristled at the thought of being succeeded by another, even if they were considered inferior. In defiance he made his own statue, and covered it all with gold, declaring, Babylon would never die; his dynasty would last forever. And to drive the point home, he called all the diplomats, the leaders, governors, and statesmen of the region to come and worship his image. Included in this bureaucratic montage were three Hebrew administrators, Shadrach, Meshach, and Abednego.

It was an imposing idol: ninety feet high, nine feet wide, and covered in pure gold. Standing on the Plain of Dura like the Eiffel Tower, or Burj Khalifa, it dwarfed everything around and reflected the sun's rays for miles. It was a beacon or "mark" of Nebuchadnezzar's power and authority. Under penalty of death, he commanded their worship.

> Then the herald loudly proclaimed, "Nations and peoples of every language, this is what you are commanded to do: As soon as you hear the sound of the horn, flute, zither, lyre, harp, pipe and all kinds of music, you must fall down and worship the image of gold that King Nebuchadnezzar has set up. Whoever does not fall down and worship will immediately be thrown into a blazing furnace."

> Therefore, as soon as they heard the sound of … music, all the nations and peoples of every language fell down and worshiped the image of gold that King Nebuchadnezzar had set up. …But there are some Jews whom you have set over the affairs of the province of Babylon—Shadrach, Meshach and Abednego—who pay no attention to you, Your Majesty. They neither serve your gods nor worship the image of gold you have set up."

> Furious with rage, Nebuchadnezzar summoned Shadrach, Meshach and Abednego. So these men were

brought before the king, and Nebuchadnezzar said to them, "Is it true, Shadrach, Meshach and Abednego that you do not serve my gods or worship the image of gold I have set up? ... But if you do not worship it, you will be thrown immediately into a blazing furnace. Then what god will be able to rescue you from my hand?"

Shadrach, Meshach and Abednego replied to him, "King Nebuchadnezzar, we do not need to defend ourselves before you in this matter. If we are thrown into the blazing furnace, the God we serve is able to deliver us from it, and he will deliver us from Your Majesty's hand. But even if he does not, we want you to know, Your Majesty, that we will not serve your gods or worship the image of gold you have set up."

Then Nebuchadnezzar was furious ..., and his attitude toward them changed. He ordered the furnace heated seven times hotter than usual and commanded some of the strongest soldiers in his army to tie [them]up ... and throw them into the blazing furnace. So these men, wearing their robes, trousers, turbans and other clothes, were bound and thrown into the blazing furnace. The king's command was so urgent and the furnace so hot that the flames of the fire killed the soldiers who took up Shadrach, Meshach and Abednego, and these three men, firmly tied, fell into the blazing furnace.

Then King Nebuchadnezzar leaped to his feet in amazement and asked his advisers, "Weren't there three men that we tied up and threw into the fire?"

They replied, "Certainly, Your Majesty."

He said, "Look! I see four men walking around in the fire, unbound and unharmed, and the fourth looks like a son of the gods."

195

Nebuchadnezzar then approached the opening of the blazing furnace and shouted, "Shadrach, Meshach and Abednego, servants of the Most High God, come out! Come here!"

So Shadrach, Meshach and Abednego came out of the fire, and the satraps, prefects, governors and royal advisers crowded around them. They saw that the fire had not harmed their bodies, nor was a hair of their heads singed; their robes were not scorched, and there was no smell of fire on them.

Then Nebuchadnezzar said, "Praise be to the God of Shadrach, Meshach and Abednego, who has sent his angel and rescued his servants! They trusted in him and defied the king's command and were willing to give up their lives rather than serve or worship any god except their own God. Therefore I decree that the people of any nation or language who say anything against the God of Shadrach, Meshach and Abednego be cut into pieces and their houses be turned into piles of rubble, for no other god can save in this way."

Then the king promoted Shadrach, Meshach and Abednego in the province of Babylon. (Dan 3:3-30)

Most commentators focus on the miraculous deliverance of God's three friends, and I don't blame them. Knowing that God watches over those that love Him is comforting indeed, especially when you are the one going through the flames, and in this case we see God Himself coming to the rescue. He didn't even send a representative. But let's take a minute and focus on Nebuchadnezzar. What kind of king would erect an image and demand that we worship it, or die, that we should fall down and give homage to him lest we be thrown into the fire to roast?

Would knowing he was generally a good person help? Ninety percent of the time Nebuchadnezzar was a saint, but not this day, not with these

Hebrew boys. Would knowing he was charismatic, gifted, musical, and brilliant at oration help; would knowing he's an un-paralleled engineer or rocket scientist do any good? Do a person's good traits need to just out-weigh his bad ones to be considered a good person? How could any person accept a forced, coerced worship? Would that be satisfying somehow? Doesn't this sound more like Satan? How can we think that Nebuchadnezzar is anything short of a despot for demanding worship under penalty of a fiery death?

If so, what about the God of the Bible? Does He say worship me or I'll kill you, like Nebuchadnezzar? Though everyone would agree that God's perfect the rest of the time, wouldn't killing people in the end with the "fires of hell" negate some of His overall goodness? I don't want to be disrespectful, but the comparison is obvious. Does God really say worship me, love me, and love each other or I'll burn you? The unequivocal answer is no. There is no way.

How did this concept ever come to be? Answer: The teaching didn't come from the Prophets and Apostles; it was incorporated into the church during the Dark Ages, in a time when superstition and ignorance ran rampant. The passionate wording of scripture, the imagery of God's amazing glory, and the description of the judgment have been misunderstood. Like I have pointed out previously, God will not turn into Nebuchadnezzar in the end.

The message we should take home from the fiery furnace is this: our Wonderful God, our Prince of Peace, our Everlasting Father saves and rescues people *out* of danger, *out* of disasters, and *out* of the "fire." He doesn't throw them in.

···◦◦◦〰〇〰◦◦◦···

CHAPTER 44

···◦◦◦〰〇〰◦◦◦···

Rest

D oes all this talk about faith and trust do away with the rules?
No, love is essential. God gave us the rules because we needed
them. But if we don't understand God's purposes in giving
them, to lead us to Christ and keep us safe, there is a great danger that
we'll become preoccupied with them and legalistic. The law is good
only if used properly, and the proper observance of the Sabbath can
express and remind each one of us of God's healing answers to the
Great Controversy. After the war started, God created our world in
six majestic days to answer the charges leveled at Him, and gave us
the Sabbath at the end of the week. Remember the Sabbath, He said.
Later, when the Israelites lost their freedom in Egypt, God came to the
rescue and gave them back their freedom, demonstrating His love and
concern, and said "add that to the Sabbath." When Jesus came to Earth
to represent the Father, most of his healings were done on the Sabbath.

And at the end of another week, Crucifixion week, after answering
the rest of the issues in the Great Controversy, Jesus Himself rested
and kept the Sabbath in the tomb. Add that to the Sabbath, He
could have said. The Sabbath, understood from a Great Controversy-
Demonstration perspective, represents all that is good about God, all
that He has said and done about the war, and how He has demonstrated
His righteousness in the conflict. In short, the Sabbath represents God's

199

answers to Satan's charges. It's not a day to be legalistically observed. It is a great blessing to those who weekly observe and remember all that God has done to demonstrate that He really is a God of love and that He loves you and me more than life itself and wants us to spend eternity with Him.

I may be wrong, but I think Jesus will come back on a Friday, and we will rest on the way up to heaven on the Sabbath. To top it off, after the judgment, when God makes all things new, He will create our planet again in the same way by taking six days, just to show us geologists that it wasn't millions or billions of years. And when He is finished, He will ask if we could all keep the next day, as a Sabbath, to remember all that has happened. When all is made new, we will take one day each week, forever, to remember what God has done to set us free.

> "From one New Moon to another and from one Sabbath to another, all mankind will come and bow down before me," says the Lord (Isa. 66:23).

CHAPTER 45

Conclusion

God has paid a huge price. Great athletes, master musicians, brain surgeons, and others who dedicate themselves to obtaining a lofty goal have paid a price. Sometimes the price is weight training for six hours a day, seven days a week, for years. Other times, it is practicing the piano and studying music theory all day, every day, for years. Prospective surgeons study relentlessly, prodigiously, just to get into medical school, spend three or four more years in school just to become a resident, then train another five to seven years, depending on their specialty, before they can do what they have dedicated themselves to do—heal people.

The price a surgeon pays is higher than most people want to afford. In comparison, what price did God pay? Who would God pay, if He had to pay someone? The phrase, "God paid the price" or "Jesus paid the price" is shorthand for remembering all the things God has done to demonstrate the truth about Himself, not the payment of a legal debt. Like the surgeon who devoted his entire life to heal and save, God, too, has devoted and dedicated Himself to the healing and saving of this planet and His universe.

God has had His reputation smeared. God has had His closest friends and millions of angels rebel against Him. He has seen billions of His children suffer with pain, sickness, disease, and death. But He has worked with every person who has ever lived to try and uplift them, and God is working with me and you right now.

God specifically watched over Israel until He could do no more for them. He fed them, nurtured them, and loved them. Then God came as Jesus, the Son. Teaching, preaching, healing, loving, giving, He gave Himself to the world, to Israel, only to be rejected. God paid, is paying, and will continue to pay every day until the war is won. And to Him it is worth it.

Jesus revealed the healing message of what the Father is really like. And to vindicate God's reputation completely, Jesus had to die, since God was accused of plotting to kill sinners and lying about sin causing death. The scripture "without the shedding of blood there can be no forgiveness of sins" is true in that, had not Jesus died to clarify the truth about God and how sinners die, and that God is worthy of our trust, we would not want to come home; we would continue our rebellion, and we wouldn't even want God's forgiveness.

After we see the truth, what God is really like and what sin really does, a truth we wouldn't have learned without seeing Jesus's humbling, awe-inspiring life and death, it is our choice to repent and be "born again." God is ready and waiting to meet us on the road back from the pigpen (Luke 15:11–31, Provonsha 1982). The legal system, with its animal sacrifices, brought us to Christ, who brought us to God, so we could be justified and saved by faith. And genuine faith is all God has ever required.

This was all a demonstration by our loving Father, a very costly manifestation that wasn't played out on a computer; it wasn't a television special with special effects and paid actors, but took God's flesh and blood and sweat and tears and unimaginable amounts of pain to demonstrate. In everything that God has done, He has been teaching us the costly truth about sin, life, death, natural consequences, wrath, fear, and what He is like. He gave us a lesson book in which His principles were demonstrated, and we were in the middle of it the entire time. To help us until we saw Jesus and heard what He had to say, we were given a lot of really good rules—a schoolmaster—to keep us safe. And because we didn't know how utterly lost we were, God used a legal model with legal language to show us our need, bring us to our knees, and lead us to Christ. But it is not that God must forgive us legally in order to be saved—it is more involved than that. He is more concerned that we're healed, born again, and want to be whole. He wants us to come home. We are the ones that need to hear that we are forgiven. We need the reassurance of His love, and He gives it freely. After faith has come, there's no more need for that aspect of the law, and no one is thinking of getting rid of love—the principle of God's universe—only the legal language normally associated with why Jesus had to die.

God has always been on our side. He is our Father, and we are his children. God (Father, Son, and Holy Spirit) initiated the whole plan together. God can forgive, and the universe will not think that He is weak or inconsistent because He demonstrated the tragic consequences of sin Himself.

God did not want us to see him as a legalist, a god who wouldn't or couldn't forgive without someone paying a legal debt, but it was a place to start. God flooded the world, killing millions, to demonstrate what couldn't be shown any other way: massive force did not rid the world of sin then, it will not now, and it will not rid the world of sin in the future. God doesn't want us to fear Him, yet God thundered at Sinai and swallowed up Korah and Dathan, just so He could save some of us. God didn't want us to divorce, but He made provision for it. God didn't want them to have a king, but He helped them find the very best. God compromised again when they wanted an intercessor. He made another concession when He let them eat clean animals. God has had to thunder at times to freeze us in our tracks long enough to give Him a second look—and live. God didn't want the Israelites to shed blood. He wanted to chase the Canaanites and other nations out of the Promised Land using hornets, but the Israelites wanted to do it the old-fashioned way, like the other nations, with blade and spear.

God was willing to pay the ultimate price. God suffered through the entire process as His relationship with the Son was destroyed. God, through Christ, suffered the terrible separation that causes death, a separation that those who trust Him will fortunately never know. And finally, even though God will never erase the past, all those who have been won back to trust in Him will be welcomed home and treated as though they have always been part of God's loyal family.

There are five specific things I want to leave you with; and as you read them consider how they make God the Father look:

1. Sin causes death—God does not kill us in the end; He only gives us up to the dreadful consequences.
2. The harsh stories of the Bible are not God's preferred methods of leadership but are demonstrations, emergency measures, and discipline, actions designed to meet us where we are and lead us a few steps closer to home.
3. Any relationship with God short of a personal, practical, trusting, and understanding friendship, in the long term, is destined to fail.
4. Force produces fear; fear produces rebellion.
5. The Bible is not just story after story leading to a final legal payment for sin. It is the unbiased history of God's answers to the issues in the war and culminates with God Himself jumping onto the train tracks, dying to vindicate His character and develop our trust.

If you listen closely, you can hear a train coming your way. Are you on the wrong tracks? Are you going the wrong way? Listen closely to your heart, and then read, compare the evidence, and pray. Many things in life are obvious, but not all. Please, consider these ideas, read your Bible over and over again, learn to read it as a whole, in context, and pray that God will help you see what is true and real.

There really is no way to properly cover these topics in so few pages. I just pray that this effort may inspire you to read the Bible again and again from a new perspective, and that you may become, if you're not already, close friends with God through Jesus Christ, the Majesty of Heaven. So which tracks are you standing on?

Part 4

Definitions

This remaining section reads more like a dictionary or encyclopedia and addresses points literally word-for-word. In the Great Controversy model, the words "gospel," "sin," "wrath," and "justice" may be used differently or given a different emphasis than is normally encountered. Although these words have been used and explained in the previous sections, some readers may still have questions regarding these commonly used, stereotypical words. I'll attempt to clarify these potential differences and then leave you with a few quotes from the greatest teacher the world has ever seen.

CHAPTER 46

The Gospel

The word "gospel," as we all know, literally means "good news," and there is a lot of good news in the Bible. The really good news is about God and how He has been shown to be true and righteous. Being saved is good news too, but the good news about God is infinitely more important. Without God being shown as righteous, there is no point in discussing our salvation. It depends on our focus. If we are totally concerned about and preoccupied with what God has done for us, then the good news is that we are going to heaven, and this is a great start. But this, though important, isn't what Paul and John meant regarding the "gospel." Paul knew his Old Testament and might have been referring to Jeremiah 9 when he penned Romans 1.

> For I am not ashamed of the gospel, because it is the power of God for the salvation of everyone who believes: first for the Jew, then for the Gentile. *For in the gospel the righteousness of God is revealed*, a righteousness that is by faith from first to last, as it is written: "The righteous will live by faith." (Rom. 1:16–17)

The reason to boast in Jeremiah—that you know Him, and He exercises kindness, justice, and righteousness—is the same as Romans

1—the righteousness of God is revealed, and it leads to ever greater faith.

Luther and others have focused on this verse regarding the righteous living by faith. But, because Luther didn't utilize the book of Revelation and its explanation of the war in heaven, he missed the connection between God being accused of wrongdoing and needing to "take his case to court." (Lutheran Church 2011)

In Revelation 14:6, John uses the term "gospel," as a reference to God's righteous character. "Then I saw another angel flying in midair, and he had the *eternal gospel* to proclaim to those who live on the earth—to every nation, tribe, language, and people."

This is the "eternal gospel." What good news has been around eternally? It has to be about God, not us being saved. It is the truth Jesus demonstrated to vindicate God's character—that God is righteous and the personification of love. He didn't lie. I don't mind if people talk about the gospel as that which God has done for us—that is good news too—but there is so much more, and it seems a waste not to expand our understanding.

---

ooo≬o00

CHAPTER 47

ooo≬0oo

Sin

The definition of "sin" is not as straightforward as you might suppose. Generally, you could say there are two kinds: original sin (the sin we are born with, an attitude of self-preservation), and the act of sin (i.e., lying, stealing, etc.). The predisposition to sin is no fault of our own, but Adam's, and the latter is the result of our own poor choices and is an inherited self-centeredness associated with our distancing ourselves from God. It is the result of not having God in our lives.

The Bible gives several definitions of sin, and many examples, such as Moses striking the rock. Many people have adopted 1 John 3:4 as their best and sometimes only definition for sin. Observe how the King James Version translates it:

Whosoever committeth sin transgresseth also the law: for sin is the transgression of the law.

Notice the emphasis is on breaking the law, which is focused on behavior. Now, compare it to other versions.

New International Version (NIV): Everyone who sins breaks the law; in fact, sin is lawlessness.

New King James Version (NKJV): Whoever commits sin also commits lawlessness; and sin is lawlessness.

New American Standard Version (NASV): Everyone who practices sin also practices lawlessness; and sin is lawlessness.

Sin is not just doing bad things, transgressing the law, breaking the rules, and stealing; it is defiance, an attitude of rebellion, and an unwillingness to conform to what's right. The last part—"sin is lawlessness"—refers to more than just making some mistakes. It implies that the sinful person is a rebel unwilling to cooperate. That is relational sin—an act of rebellion. In the Greek, however, the complication goes away. It just says, sin is lawlessness. Young's Literal Translation puts it this way:

Everyone who is doing the sin, the lawlessness also he doth do, and the sin is the lawlessness.

Another definition of sin is given in Romans:

And everything that does not come from faith is sin. (Rom. 14:23)

People with faith trust God; People who sin fear God. It can be stated different ways, but at the core, those who fear God are sinning even if they have not lied, stolen, or committed adultery. So often we attach our actions with the word sin, but sin has different meanings and connotations. Fearing our perfect God is damaging.

Romans 14:23 gets to the heart of relational sin. What went wrong in the beginning? Wasn't it the breakdown of trust? What does God want from His creatures? Habakkuk, Hebrews, and Romans all point us to faith and trust—the opposite of sin. Faith and sin are polar opposites.

Here is another definition for sin:

James 4:17 (NKJV) says, Therefore, to him who knows to do good and does not do it, to him it is sin.

Not only does this verse talk about an action that didn't happen, it also describes an attitude in which we know what our duty is, yet we consciously choose not to do it. This is another form of rebellion—no trust, no faith, no respect, and no love. Remember Moses's sin at the rock. Did God say, "Moses, the reason you are not going into the Promised Land is because you disobeyed?" No. God said, "Because you didn't believe Me, trust Me, or have faith in Me."

> But the Lord said to Moses and Aaron, "Because you did not *trust* in me enough to honor me as holy in the sight of the Israelites, you will not bring this community into the land I give them." (Num. 20:12)

Notice the difference in the New Living Version:

> But the Lord said to Moses and Aaron, "Because you did not *trust* me enough to *demonstrate* my holiness to the people of Israel, you will not lead them into the land I am giving them!" (Num. 20:12)

In conclusion, sin is not merely breaking the rules, although breaking the rules is indeed sin. The greatest sin—the *big sin*—the sin that leads to all other sins, is our broken relationship with God; it's rebelling, being fearful, telling God no, and it is caused by believing Satan's lies. When that sin is corrected—when we are brought back to love, trust, and admire our God—then the other sins will go away. We won't need to protect our fragile egos. We must address the relational atonement first. Otherwise, we may only create a legalistic, outward, behavioral change without an accompanying change in heart.

CHAPTER **48**

Wrath and Paraditimy (To Deliver)

- The Lord hardened Pharaoh's heart (Exod. 20:10);
  - Pharaoh hardened his [Pharaoh's] heart (Exod. 8:32, KJV).
- So the Lord put him to death [Saul] … (1 Chron. 10:14, KJV)
  - So Saul took his own sword and fell on it. (1 Sam. 31:4, NIV)
- Again the anger of the Lord burned against Israel, and he incited David against them, saying, "Go and take a census of Israel and Judah." (2 Sam. 24:1)
  - Satan rose up against Israel and incited David to take a census of Israel (1 Chron. 21:1)

Who killed Saul: God or Saul? Who hardened Pharaoh's heart: God or Pharaoh? Who incited David to number Israel? The Lord or Satan? Who let Sampson be taken captive: God, Sampson, or Delilah? Who allowed the Jewish temple to be sacked in AD 70: God or the Israelites who rejected Him? In all cases, the answer could be God, because God stopped protecting His people from their poor choices—He let them go, He gave them up, He delivered them over—but it can also be said that they did it themselves, that they had it coming.

In each situation, there was a choice to be made: stay with God and receive His associated protection and blessings, or reject God and go solo. And in each case, the person or group of people chose to go it alone, and the consequences were severe.

Who really killed Saul? Saul. Who hardened Pharaoh's heart? Pharaoh. The Bible tells the story both ways. Did God do that to confuse or mystify us? No. Different Bible writers emphasize different parts of the story. Because God is sovereign, and He shapes events, He makes us choose, and in the case of Pharaoh, God made him choose whether he would let Israel go, and he didn't. With Saul, God would have taken care of him in battle, but Saul rejected God; and consequently, God left him to defend himself. Likewise with David, God allowed David to go it alone—that was what David wanted to do, and Satan was more than willing to help David down that path. Without God's protection, Saul was wounded by the Philistines, and fell on his sword, killing himself, to keep from being tortured. God set up the circumstances, but Saul and Pharaoh made the choices. Thus it can be said both ways—God killed Saul and Saul killed himself.

This can be applied to the judgment and the second death, too. The Bible alludes to God actively punishing in the end, pouring out His wrath, but like these other stories, we are ultimately responsible.

Let's consider God's wrath and the third angel's message from Revelation Chapter 14.

> A third angel followed them and said in a loud voice: "If anyone worships the beast and its image and receives its mark on their forehead or on their hand, they, too, will drink the wine of God's fury, which has been poured full strength into the cup of his wrath. They will be tormented with burning sulfur in the presence of the holy angels and of the Lamb. And the smoke of their torment will rise forever and ever. There will be no rest day or night for those who worship the beast and its image, or for anyone who receives the mark of its name. (Rev. 14:9–12)

There is not a more terrifying passage in the Bible, and it certainly appears as though God is angry. But can you imagine gentle Jesus doing this, the One who died to reveal the truth about God? We certainly don't want to forget the lessons we learned by watching Jesus die. This wrathful message is God's last attempt to get our attention; it's the last chance for planet Earth, and God wants us to take notice and prepare for His coming. God lets us reap what we have sown. He is actually weeping over us like when he cried over Jerusalem. In chapter 27 I presented the cup of God's wrath, and it is clear Jesus drank that cup to the bottom; He experienced God's wrath, but what happened? Was there fire and brimstone?

Consider the following. God's wrath is discussed in Romans 1 and is equated to Jesus's death in Romans 4.

> [1:18] The **wrath of God** is being revealed from heaven against all the godlessness and wickedness of people, who suppress the truth by their wickedness.
>
> [24] Therefore **God gave them over** in the sinful desires of their hearts to sexual impurity for the degrading of their bodies with one another. [25] They exchanged the truth about God for a lie.
>
> [26] Because of this, **God gave them over** to shameful lusts.
>
> [28] Furthermore, just as they did not think it worthwhile to retain the knowledge of God, so **God gave them over** to a depraved mind,
>
> [4:24] but also for us, to whom God will credit righteousness—for us who believe in him who raised Jesus our Lord from the dead. [25] **He was delivered over** to death for our sins and was raised to life for our justification.

In Romans 1: 24, 26, 28 and 4:25: Paraditomy, or its root word, is used every time. Look below at what it looks like in Greek. Each text comes from Stephens 1550 Textus Receptus, and the word paraditomy is shown in bold type.

1:24

διο και ***παρεδωκεν*** αυτουςο θεοςεν ταις επιθυμιαις των καρδιων αυτων εις ακαθαρσιαν του ατιμαζεσθ αι τα σωματα αυτωα εν εαυτιοσ

1:26

δια τουτο ***παρεδωκεν*** *αυτους* ο θεος εις παθη ατιμιας αι τε γαρ θηλειαι αυτων μετηλλαξαν την φυσικην χρησιν εις την παρα φυσιν

1:28

και καθως ουκ εδοκιμασαν τον θεον εχειν εν επιγνωσει ***παρεδωκεν*** *αυτους* ο θεος εις αδοκιμον νουν ποιειν τα μη καθηκοντα

4:25

ος ***παρεδοθη*** δια τα παραπτωματα ημων καί ηγερθη δια την δικαιωσιν ημων

A detailed reading of the Bible should verify there are a least two types of "wrath," just as there are multiple definitions of "sin" and "gospel." Sometimes, God does work on our level, and He says things that may seem harsh or angry, but He does so to get a specific result, like when we discipline our children. God is never angry in the way that we get angry, and He is always under control. Nothing happens that He has not foreseen, for God knows the end from the beginning.

The second type of wrath, the wrath that culminates in the second death, is the wrath demonstrated when God sadly gives up a person or people. God reluctantly handed His people over to the natural consequences many times.

The Minor Prophets—Hosea, Amos, Micah, and Zephaniah— make this clear, as does Romans 1. God will let people suffer the consequences of their choices:

> There is no faithfulness, no love, no *acknowledgment of God* in the land ... my people are destroyed *from lack of knowledge*. Because you have *rejected knowledge*, I also

> reject you as my priests. ... *Ephraim is joined to idols: leave him alone!* (Hosea 4:1, 6, 17).
>
> For I desire mercy, not sacrifice, and acknowledgment of God rather than burnt offerings. (Hosea 6:6)
>
> How can I give you up, Ephraim? How can I hand you over, Israel? How can I treat you like Sodom? How can I make you like Gomorrah? My heart is changed within me; all my compassion is aroused. I will not carry out my fierce anger, nor will I turn and devastate Ephraim, for I am God, and not man—the Holy One among you. I will not come in wrath. (Hosea 11:8–9)

God allowed the people to go into captivity. God gave them up to the natural consequences of their choices. He chose to no longer work with them and shield them from their enemies. Paul picked up on this same theme after discussing the righteousness of God in Romans chapter 1:

> The wrath of God is being revealed from heaven against all the godlessness and wickedness of men who suppress the truth by their wickedness. ... *Therefore God gave them over* in the sinful desires of their hearts. ... They exchanged the truth of God for a lie, and worshiped and served created things rather than the Creator. ... Because of this, *God gave them over* to shameful lusts. ... Furthermore, since they did not think it worthwhile to retain the knowledge of God, *He gave them over* to a depraved mind. (Rom. 1:18, 24–26, 28)

Jesus too calls out on the cross, "My God, My God, why have you forsaken me?" (Matt. 27:46, NIV), the same wording as in Psalms 22: 1–2 and in Hosea 11:8 when God describes His wrath. Jesus suffered the wrath of God and died alone and heartbroken. Jesus tells us in Matthew 23 that He would love to have taken care of His people like a hen covers her chicks, but they wouldn't have Him, so He had to let them go. "Oh Jerusalem, Jerusalem, you who kill the prophets and stoned those sent to you, how often I have longed to gather your children together, as a hen gathers her chicks under her wings, but you were not willing. Look, your house is left to you *desolate"* (Matt. 23:37–38). What else can a loving God do who totally respects His creatures' freedom and individuality? How can you command love? You can only invite love. Like friendship, love cannot be forced or commanded, and only by love is love awakened.

This is a window to the larger view. You can demand or command obedience, but you cannot command the things that God wants the most. *You cannot command love.* Does God really say that if you don't love Him "with all your heart, with all your soul, with all your strength, and with all your mind," (Luke 10:27) that He will destroy you in the judgment—love Me, or I'll kill you? That makes no sense. If it is true that what God wants most is love, and because love cannot be commanded, then the death God spoke of in the beginning must be one of natural consequences, not an imposed punishment. For if it is an imposed punishment, then there cannot be pure love, for fear will be mixed in. Perfect love casts out all fear. "There is no fear in love. But perfect love drives out fear, because fear has to do with punishment. The one who fears is not made perfect in love" (1 John 4:8).

CHAPTER 49

—◦◦○ ◦○◦—

Words from Jesus

Jesus's words are not like Paul's or Luke's or Peter's, or even John's. Jesus's words are simple, direct, and unassuming. Does that mean that Jesus never spoke about the atonement, justification, or sanctification; did He forget to explain propitiation, expiation, and whether grace is imparted or imputed? He addressed all of these topics, but He was speaking to a different audience with different needs, so the language isn't the same as these other men used. Jesus could explain the most difficult concepts in such a way that no one had to consult a dictionary when He was finished, yet he spoke to the most learned and the most unpretentious. Jesus spoke to humble fishermen and craftsmen; He taught the lame and those in pain, and at times even lawyers and governors, but He always had the right words. Jesus addressed all these topics, but for some unknown reason we have preferred the more complicated speech of the apostles. What did Jesus say? What do we need to do to be saved? In reply Jesus declared, "I tell you the truth, no one can see the kingdom of God unless he is *born again*" (John 3:3).

How does Jesus save us?

> For God so loved the world that he gave his one and
> only Son, that whoever believes in him shall not perish
> but have eternal life. For God did not send his Son into

the world to condemn the world, but to save the world through him. *Whoever believes in him is not condemned,* but whoever does not believe stands condemned already because he has not believed in the name of God's one and only Son. This is the verdict: *Light has come into the world,* but men loved darkness instead of light because their deeds were evil. Everyone who does evil hates the light, and will not come into the light for fear that his deeds will be exposed. But whoever lives by the **truth** comes into the light, so that it may be seen plainly that what he has done has been done through God. (John 3:16–21)

What is the atonement about?

My prayer is not for them alone. I pray also for those who will believe in me through their message, that all of them may be one, Father, just as you are in me and I am in you. May they also be in us so that the world may believe that you have sent me. I have given them the glory that you gave me, that they may be one as we are one: I in them and you in me. May they be brought to complete unity to let the world know that you sent me and have loved them even as you have loved me. "Father, I want those you have given me to be with me where I am, and to see my glory, the glory you have given me because you loved me before the creation of the world. Righteous Father, though the world does not know you, I know you, and they know that you have sent me. I have made you known to them, and will continue to make you known in order that the love you have for me may be in them and that I myself may be in them." (John 17:20–26)

Jesus's responses are not as legal as we usually describe them. They are relational, logical, and natural.

Works Cited

"Arbitrary, Exacting, Severe." *Merriam-Webster.com*. 2011. http://www.merriam-webster.com. (Accessed May 21, 2011)

"Canon." Bible Researcher. http://www.bibleresearcher.com. (Accessed June 3, 2011)

Edwards, Mark Jr. 1995–2008. "Apocalypticism Explained: Martin Luther." *Apocalypse: The Evolution of Apocalyptic Belief and How It Shaped the Western World*. http://www.pbs.org/wgbh/pages/frontline/shows/apocalypse/explanation/martinluther.html. (Accessed May 21, 2010)

GreatSite Marketing. 1997–2008. "English Bible History: Martin Luther." http://www.greatsite.com/timeline-englishbible-history/martin-luther.html. (Accessed May 21, 2010)

Hartin, Patrick J. 2003. *James*. Sacra Pagina Commentary Series V.14 Collegeville, MN. http://catholicbooksreview.org/2010/hartin.htm. (Accessed May 21, 2010)

Lutheran Church, Our Savior. *Luther's Teaching*. 1029 Sixth St., Port Huron, MI 48060. http://oursaviourlutheran.com/new_page_6.htm. (Accessed June 6, 2011)

Maxwell, Graham. 1992. *Servants or Friends*. Redlands, CA: Pine Knoll Publications.

————. 2002. *Can God Be Trusted?* Redlands, CA: Pine Knoll Publications.

Marsh, Ernest C. 2010. English Translation of the Greek Septuagint Bible The Translation of the Greek Old Testament Scriptures, Including the Apocrypha. *Compiled from the Translation by Sir Lancelot C. L. Brenton, 1851* http://ecmarsh.com/lxx/lxx_account. html Presented by The Common Man's Prospective. Copyright© 1999–2010 Ernest C. Marsh

MSG NavPress, a division of The Navigators, USA. Originally published by NavPress in English as THE MESSAGE: The Bible in Contemporary Language, copyright 2002, by Eugene Peterson. All rights reserved. http://www.biblestudytools.com/msg

Provonsha, Jack. 1982. *You Can Go Home Again*. Washington, DC: Review and Herald.

Rodkinson, Michael, L. 1918. *The Babylonian Talmud*. Vols. 1–10. http://www.ultimatebiblereferencelibrary.com Talmud Translated by Michael L. Rodkinson.pdf. (Accessed June 4, 2011)

Roth, Steven. 2000. "What's So New about the New Covenant?" Unpublished manuscript.

Septuagint online. http://www.kalvesmaki.com/lxx/. (Accessed June 3, 2011)

Photo Credits

Front Cover, http://www.thinkstockphotos.com/image/stock-photo-jesus-walking-on-the water/99104516/

Page 2, http://www.123rf.com/photo_12774226_the-front-facade-and-courtyard-of-the-library-building-at-ephesus-turkey.html'>searagen / 123RF Stock Photo

Page 6, http://www.biblegallery.com/contact.html Bible Gallery.com 55 West Oak Ridge Dr., Hagerstown, MD 21740; 301-393-3211

Page 15, http://www.123rf.com/photo_8890591_europe-relief-from-space-earth-map-from-nasa.html'>1xpert / 123RF Stock Photo

Page 26, http://www.123rf.com/photo_16224842_sacrifices-driven-out-of-eden--picture-from-the-holy-scriptures-old-and-new-testaments-books-collect.html'>nicku / 123RF Stock Photo

Page 34, http://www.123rf.com/photo_12994077_the-tower-of-babel-1-le-sainte-bible-traduction-nouvelle-selon-la-vulgate-par-mm-j-j-bourasse-et-p-j.html'>ruskpp / 123RF Stock Photo

Page 44, http://www.123rf.com/photo_16224824_the-testing-of-abraham-s-faith--picture-from-the-holy-scriptures-old-and-new-testaments-books-collec.html'>nicku / 123RF Stock Photo

Page 51, http://www.123rf.com/photo_16225140_the-giving-of-the-law-upon-mt-sinai--picture-from-the-holy-scriptures-old-and-new-testaments-books-c.html'>nicku / 123RF Stock Photo

Page 61, http://www.123rf.com/photo_16225119_moses-striking-the-rock-in-horeb--picture-from-the-holy-scriptures-old-and-new-testaments-books-coll.html'>nicku / 123RF Stock Photo

Page 65, http://www.123rf.com/photo_16224859_the-israelite-discovers-his-concubine-dead--picture-from-the-holy-scriptures-old-and-new-testaments-.html'>nicku/123RF Stock Photo

Page 86, http://www.123rf.com/photo_16102385_jesus-with-the-doctors--picture-from-the-holy-scriptures-old-and-new-testaments-books-collection-pub.html'>nicku / 123RF Stock Photo

Page 88, http://www.123rf.com/photo_16225078_jesus-and-the-woman-at-the-well--picture-from-the-holy-scriptures-old-and-new-testaments-books.html'>nicku / 123RF Stock Photo

Page 100, http://www.123rf.com/photo_16102232_jesus-and-the-woman-taken-in-adultery--picture-from-the-holy-scriptures-old-and-new-testaments-books.html'>nicku / 123RF Stock Photo

Page 104, http://www.123rf.com/photo_16102362_the-buyers-and-sellers-driven-out-of-the-temple--picture-from-the-holy-scriptures-old-and-new-testam.html'>nicku / 123RF Stock Photo

Page 107, http://www.123rf.com/photo_16102222_the-agony-in-the-garden--picture-from-the-holy-scriptures-old-and-new-testaments-books-collection-pu.html'>nicku / 123RF Stock Photo

Page 114, http://www.123rf.com/photo_12994078_the-death-of-jesus-1-le-sainte-bible-traduction-nouvelle-selon-la-vulgate-par-mm-j-j-bourasse-et-p-j.html'>ruskpp / 123RF Stock Photo

Page 120, http://www.123rf.com/photo_16094241_an-angel-announces-to-the-women-that-jesus-has-risen--picture-from-the-holy-scriptures-old-and-new-t.html'>nicku/123RF Stock Photo

Page 151, http://www.123rf.com/photo_16224831_jesus-healing-the-demoniac-boy--picture-from-the-holy-scriptures-old-and-new-testaments-books-collec.html'>nicku / 123RF Stock Photo

Page 164, http://www.123rf.com/photo_12994086_moses-and-the-commandments-1-le-sainte-bible-traduction-nouvelle-selon-la-vulgate-par-mm-j-j-bourass.html'>ruskpp / 123RF Stock Photo</a>

Page 170, http://www.123rf.com/photo_16224874_the-death-of-samson--picture-from-the-holy-scriptures-old-and-new-testaments-books-collection-publis.html'>nicku / 123RF Stock Photo

Page 182, http://www.123rf.com/photo_16224984_conversion-of-saul-picture-from-the-holy-scriptures-old-and-new-testaments-books-collection-publish.html'>nicku / 123RF Stock Photo

Page 192, http://www.123rf.com/photo_16102225_Shadrach, Meshach, and Abednego in the Fiery Furnace-picture –from-the-holy-scriptures-old-and-new-testaments-books-collection-publish. html'>nicku/123RF Stock Photo

Page 198, http://www.123rf.com/photo_16225017_the-new-jerusalem-picture-from-the-holy-scriptures-old-and-new-testaments-books-collection-publishe.html'>nicku / 123RF Stock Photo

Suggested Reading and Sources

Cinquemani, Paul. 2007. *Oh My God!* Kearney, NE: Morris Publishing.

Jennings, Timothy R. 2007. *Could It Be This Simple? A Biblical Model for Healing the Mind.* Hagerstown, MD: Review and Herald, Autumn House.

Maxwell, Graham. 1992. *Servants or Friends.* Redlands, CA: Pine Knoll Publications.

———. 2002. *Can God Be Trusted?* Redlands, CA: Pine Knoll Publications.

Pine Knoll Ministry. http://www.pineknoll.org/.

Provonsha, Jack. 1982. *You Can Go Home Again.* Washington, DC: Review and Herald.

Vendon, Morris. 1986. *How Jesus Treated People.* Nampa, ID: Pacific Press.

———. 1986. *A Lonely Planet.* Nampa, ID: Pacific Press.

About the Author

C hris Conrad earned a bachelor's degree from Colorado State University and a master's degree from Wichita State University in geology. He has taught math, science, and the Bible and has led Bible studies for the past thirty years. Conrad specializes in creation vs. evolution issues and is a professional geologist in Utah.